Syria

Syria

David W. Lesch

Polity

First published in 2019 by Polity Press

Polity Press
65 Bridge Street
Cambridge CB2 1UR, UK

Polity Press
101 Station Landing
Suite 300
Medford, MA 02155, USA

ISBN-13: 978-1-5095-2751-9
ISBN-13: 978-1-5095-2752-6 (pb)

A catalogue record for this book is available from the British Library.

Library of Congress Cataloging-in-Publication Data

Names: Lesch, David W., author.
Title: Syria / David W. Lesch.
Description: Cambridge, UK : Polity Press, 2019. | Includes bibliographical
    references and index.
Identifiers: LCCN 2018032455 (print) | LCCN 2018034955 (ebook) | ISBN
    9781509527557 (Epub) | ISBN 9781509527519 | ISBN 9781509527519(hardback)
    | ISBN 9781509527526(pbk.)
Subjects: LCSH: Syria--History--20th century. | Syria--History--21st century.
Classification: LCC DS95 (ebook) | LCC DS95 .L47 2019 (print) | DDC
    956.9104--dc23
LC record available at https://lccn.loc.gov/2018032455

Typeset in 11 on 13 Berkeley by
Servis Filmsetting Ltd, Stockport, Cheshire
Printed and bound by CPI Group (UK) Ltd, Croydon, CR0 4YY

For further information on Polity, visit our website: politybooks.com

Contents

A Political Map of Syria

Preface

Syria has become something of a second home for me. Since my first visit to the country in 1989 to conduct research on my dissertation, I have visited it over thirty times, staying for months at a time on occasion. I have, therefore, come to know Syria quite well for a Westerner, often learning about the country from the inside out. Although nothing compared to the suffering of Syrians today, it has been one of the most difficult periods of my life to see a number of friends and acquaintances on both sides of the conflict having been killed or displaced as the result of the civil war that has raged since 2011. One of those people was Dr. Khalid al-Asaad, the Head of Antiquities of the magnificent Roman era ruins at Palmyra. Dr. Khalid had personally escorted me and my family around Palmyra on multiple occasions. When the Islamic State of Iraq and Syria (ISIS) took over the city from Syrian government forces, he decided to stay rather than flee, as most of its inhabitants had done. It appears Dr. Khalid remained because he wanted to try to do what he could to preserve the ruins and museum against the inclination of ISIS to destroy anything that was pre- or non-Islamic. After about a month of ISIS occupation, Dr. Khalid was beheaded at age eighty-two. Thereafter ISIS went on to damage and destroy a number of priceless ruins.

Stories of suffering and senseless violence such as this unfortunately are too numerous to count. I have tried to do what I can since the beginning of the civil war to facilitate conflict resolution and/or create the parameters for political dialogue between opposing sides. I developed and organized (along with William Ury) the Harvard University–NUPI (Norwegian Institute of International Affairs)–Trinity University Syria Research Project, funded by the governments of Norway and Switzerland. I led a team of researchers in 2012–13 to meet with most of the stakeholders in the Syrian conflict in and outside of Syria, including many Syrian armed opposition leaders and Syrian government officials. The data provided necessary insights into the dynamics of the conflict in order to formulate possible pathways toward conflict resolution. In fall 2013 we completed a final report for the project and presented our findings at the highest levels in Europe, the United States, and at the United Nations (an abridged version is available at the link listed in Chapter 8, note 2). In 2014–16 I engaged in what essentially became phase two of the project, Trinity partnering in this instance with Conflict Dynamics International or CDI (based in Cambridge, MA) and funded by the Danish government. We continued our efforts at finding common ground among the combatants. In 2017 I began working with The Carter Center and CDI on an initiative along similar lines, and it is currently ongoing as of this writing. As such, I have had the opportunity to observe at close quarters many aspects of the Syrian civil war, which, I believe, has only enhanced my understanding and, hopefully, my portrayal of it, for instance in my book *Syria: The Fall of the House of Assad* (2013), and subsequent writings and commentaries.

Finally, as is well known, I met regularly with Syrian President Bashar al-Assad and many other leading Syrian officials between 2004 and 2009, first conducting research for what would become the book *The New Lion of Damascus: Bashar al-Asad and Modern Syria* (2005), and thereafter in mostly futile attempts to improve US–Syria relations. However, again, it provided me with a uniquely close vantage point from which to view the inner workings of the Syrian government and its president. Hopefully, in this book, I have been able to translate all of these experiences into a better understanding of a country for which and a people for whom I have great affection.

I would like to thank Polity Press, and its editor, Dr. Louise Knight, for approaching me in 2017 with this opportunity. It is a book I have long thought about writing, that is, a general, accessible history of modern Syria, but for one reason or another, mostly because of my involvement in various diplomatic initiatives, I was not able to do so. Since this volume is by design a concise history of modern Syria, I had to perform triage at times on what or what not to include, so this is by no means an exhaustive treatment of the subject.

It has been a pleasure to work with Louise as well as her assistant editor, Nekane Tanaka Galdos, production editor Rachel Moore, copy-editor Justin Dyer, and the whole Polity Press production team. Finally, I would not be able to do anything of any note without the love and support of my wife, Judy Dunlap, through whom everything I do flows.

For the people of Syria . . .

1

What is Syria?

Syria is a country today known for all the wrong reasons: civil war, vicious sectarianism, rampant death and destruction, a massive refugee exodus, terrorism, and so on. It is a fractured mosaic. But how did it come to this? There were, of course, immediate causes of the current civil war that are related to the so-called "Arab Spring" that spread across much of the Middle East in 2010–11. In addition, there were conditions indigenous to Syria that generated the initial uprising. However, there are also long-term causes and historical forces that have been at work in the country for decades, reaching back to the days of the Ottoman empire in the nineteenth century. But modern Syria owes most of its formative roots to the World War I, mandate, and post-independence periods in the twentieth century. This book will outline this historical trajectory of Syria, from a rich, multi-cultural historical blend to European-imposed artificiality, and from post-independence political and geo-strategic struggles to a one-party, military dictatorship, a socio-economic and political milieu from which emerged a tragic civil war.

The diversity in the country today is born out of centuries of influences near and far. The region traditionally known as Syria has been something of an amorphous entity generally located in the area we geographically know currently as the Syrian Arab Republic. Syria scholar Christopher Phillips conducted an informal poll in Syria on the question of identity given to a couple of hundred respondents a few years before the outbreak of the civil war in 2011.[1] The question was the following: Do you think of yourself first as a Syrian, an Arab, or a Muslim? Interestingly, the responses were divided about evenly between all three. Notably, however, no one listed the Syrian identity lower than second. So while this informal poll suggests that there are still multiple primary identities in Syria, the concept of a Syrian state and a Syrian nationality has taken hold in the country since independence in 1946. As we shall see, some of this has been force-fed by authoritarian fiat (it is, after all, the Syrian *Arab* Republic), but it may be instructive to the future reconstitution of a broken state when the war ends and the rebuilding begins in earnest.

All of this is indicative of how identity (or the lack thereof) has played such an important role in Syrian history – and it is clearly an unfinished story. Thus, the modern history of Syria will be placed within the context of these (and some other) identities as they have developed in concert with and in opposition to each other over the years amid a complex multidimensional matrix of domestic, regional, and international politics.

The Historical and Physical Setting

Geographically, Syria measures 71,504 square miles (185,170 square kilometers), including the Israeli-occupied Golan (*Jawlan*) Heights, which lies about thirty-five kilometers from Damascus at its closest point – all in all Syria is about the size of North Dakota. This is, however, the modern nation-state of Syria, whose name is most likely derived from the great pre-Common Era Middle Eastern kingdom of Assyria. The Romans called this area of the Fertile Crescent, an agriculturally rich area north of the Arabian desert arcing from present-day Israel/ Palestine and Lebanon to the Tigris–Euphrates area, "Suri," from old Babylonian.[2] Many Syrians consider the modern boundaries of their country to be but a rump of the whole, an arbitrary European-designed portion of what generally is thought of as greater Syria (*Bilad al-Sham*), which also consists of present-day Lebanon, Jordan, Israel, including the occupied territories, and parts of southern Turkey. In the West, this area of the Middle East became known as the Levant, an Italian word used by traders to mean "the point where the sun rises."[3] These areas are thought to have been artificially separated from Syria as a result of the post-World War I mandate system manufactured by Europe.

Syria today is a primarily semi-arid and desert plateau, with a narrow coastal plain along the Mediterranean Sea. The Syrian desert, in essence the northern extension of the Arabian desert, abuts deeply into this portion of the country. As such, nearly eighty percent of all Syrians live in the western twenty percent of the country, what the French mandate authorities initially – and somewhat derisively – called "useful Syria." The bulk of this concentration of people live in a north–south line of cities (Aleppo, Hama, Homs, Damascus) that generally separates the more fertile areas of the country from the semi-arid and desert plain. The borders that became modern Syria cut off many parts of the country from their traditional mercantile and cultural links. For example, Damascus traditionally looked toward the Mediterranean through Beirut and Haifa (Israel) as well as to the desert toward Baghdad; whereas Aleppo, heavily influenced by its proximity to Turkish, Armenian, and Kurdish areas, tended to look to the Mediterranean as well, but it also leaned eastward, as it was a critical way station along the silk route to Central Asia. It is little wonder then that there are a number of cross-cultural affinities and ties. These cross-cultural identities have had political implications – and produced irredentist claims – over the years that have at times complicated Syria's relations with its neighbors.

The arable land amounts to about one-quarter of the total. The agricultural sector produces high quantities of cotton, wheat, barley, sugar beet, and olives. Although eighty percent of Syria's agriculture is rain-fed, the government in the decade prior to the 2011 uprising had invested heavily in developing irrigation systems in order to maintain crop production during drought years. Rainfall is seasonal in Syria, most of it coming in the winter months and falling in the northern- and western-most parts of the country. Syria – as well as other parts of the Middle East – had been suffering for about two decades from drought-like conditions, which particularly decimated the agrarian sector in the rural areas of the country and contributed in some important ways to the growing discontent that underpinned the nature of the uprising itself.

It is difficult to estimate the current population of Syria because of the population shifts caused by the war. The population before the war was a little over twenty-two million, about forty percent of whom were below the age of fourteen. About half of the country's population as of this writing are displaced either externally or internally, with about five hundred thousand estimated to have been killed. Before the war, the capital and largest city in Syria, Damascus, had a population of approximately five million, Aleppo had 4.5 million, Homs (Hims) 1.8 million, Hama 1.6 million, and Latakia one million. However, because of the destruction levels and intensity of conflict in a number of Syrian cities, particularly in Aleppo and Homs, these numbers have dramatically changed. The populations of Damascus proper, as well as of cities such as Latakia and Tartus, which have for the most part remained securely under Syrian government control during the war, have risen quite substantially with the influx of displaced persons seeking refuge from the conflict. Such is the difficulty of applying numbers to today's Syria that the United Nations essentially gave up the number estimate business a few years into the conflict because of the paucity of independent reporting and lack of access due to security concerns.

Approximately ninety percent of the population is Arab, including some four hundred thousand Palestinian refugees. Arabic is thus the official and most widely spoken language. The Kurds make up about five to ten percent of the population depending upon the source. Many of the Kurds still speak Kurdish and most live in the northeast portion of the country, although there are sizeable numbers who reside in the major cities. Armenians (clustered primarily in and around Aleppo) and a smattering of other groups, such as Turkomans, Circassians, and Jews, make up the remaining small percentage of the population.

Sunni Muslims account for about seventy-five percent of the population (with Sunni *Arab* Muslims constituting sixty-five percent), and they are the majority in every province of Syria save for Latakia and Suwayda. The Alawites (see below) number approximately twelve percent of the population, and they form the majority (about sixty-two percent) in the province of Latakia; indeed, seventy-five percent of them reside there.[4] Christians of various sects, although the largest is Greek Orthodox, come in at about ten percent, and the Druze constitute about three percent, most of whom are located in southwestern Syria in the Suwayda province (about eighty-seven percent of the province, also referred to as the Jabal al-Druze or Jabal al-Arab). There is also, as noted above, a very small Jewish population, which, together with some other small Muslim sects, such as the Ismailis, represent one to three percent. The apportionment of minority populations shifted in and after the 1960s once the Baath Party, itself disproportionately comprised of minority groups in power positions, such as Alawites and Druze, came to power in 1963. With the coming of this more favorable political and economic environment, many began to migrate to the cities from the rural areas where they had been confined for centuries. Again, all these numbers have probably shifted to a degree due to the conflict, with so many Syrians, about 4.5 million, now residing as refugees outside of the country and many internally displaced persons moving to different cities inside the country to escape conflict. There will need to be a thorough and independent census taken in Syria after the war ends, including a determination of how many current refugees decided to repatriate.

The Alawites are an obscure offshoot of Twelver Shiite Islam, although a number of Alawi religious figures might argue this point, instead saying that Alawites constitute a distinct branch of Islam rather than a schism of mainstream Shiism. Alawites venerate Ali ibn Abi Talib as the "bearer of divine essence," second in importance only to the Prophet Muhammad himself. Ali was the son-in-law and cousin of Muhammad, the fourth caliph or successor to the Prophet as the leader of the Islamic community, and one of the seminal figures in Islamic history. The name "Alawite" or "Alawi" translates into "those who follow Ali." Also known as Nusayris, a name derived from a ninth-century Muslim prophet, Muhammad ibn Nusayr al-Namiri, the Alawites integrate some Christian and even Persian Zoroastrian rituals and holidays into their faith. For this reason, Sunni Muslims and even most Shiite Muslims have considered Alawite Islam to be heretical. The great thirteenth- and fourteenth-century Sunni Islamic scholar Ibn Taymiyya issued a fatwa (religious ruling) calling the Alawites greater infidels than Christians, Jews, or idolaters, and he authorized a *jihad* (struggle or holy war) against them.

Until recent times, then, the Alawites in Syria, located primarily in the northwestern reaches of the country, had been a persecuted minority for centuries. It has been traditionally thought that the Alawites – as well as some other minority religious groups – took refuge in mountainous regions of the country to escape persecution by the Sunni Muslim majority. Indicative of their subject status, as noted by Nikolaos van Dam, is the fact that well into the twentieth century, the poorest Alawi families "indentured their daughters as house servants to the richer families, mostly urban Sunnis, who usually regarded the Alawi peasants with contempt."[5] In part this may be the case, but it just as well could be that, as Patrick Seale once stated, the Alawites, Druze, and Ismailis are "a remnant of the Shi'i upsurge, which had swept Islam a thousand years before: they were islands left by a tide that receded."[6] Seale is referring to the so-called "Shiite century," which roughly lasted from the mid-tenth to the mid-eleventh centuries, when the Ismaili Shiite (or Sevener) Fatimid empire ruled over Egypt and Syria, and the Iraq- and Iran-based Buyid (Buwayhid) confederacy, under whose patronage Twelver Shiite (*Ithna ashari*) Islam developed, held sway in the heart of the Islamic world. Geography, religion, and ethnicity tended to intermix and produce identifiable pockets of sectarian and ethnic distinction that produced strong communal bonds.

Alongside these ethnic, regional, and religious identities, there exist tribal and family allegiances and alliances that have also played an important role historically. Indeed, for much of Syrian history prior to its formation as a nation-state, most in Syria would identify primarily by their family or tribal affiliation, especially outside of the larger cities. In the cities themselves, tribal and family identification receded into the modern period as new socio-economic relationships, political identification and ideologies, and the enhanced mobility commensurate with modernity muddied the waters of traditional connections, but they were still important, and remain so even to this day; indeed, as political and economic power coalesced around a select group of clans in Syria in the nineteenth and into the twentieth centuries, familial connections continued to be barometers of influence. For those from one of the main cities in Syria, you were just as likely to hear someone identify themselves as *Halabi* (*Halab* or Aleppo), Damascene, Homsi (from Homs), and so on. Indeed, there remains an urban–rural divide in Syria that has often taken on sectarian dimensions and has played a very important role in modern Syrian history.

In fact, identities in Syria were often layered and crisscrossing. The formation of the nation-state in the twentieth century as well as the rise of political Islam and Arab nationalist ideologies only added more layers to the nature of Syrian identity.

The Historical Syrian Mosaic

The area we know as Syria today is rich in cultural traditions. It is a true crossroads of history. Many different empires, peoples, and cultures have traversed this territory for millennia, usually on the road to conquest or fleeing would-be conquerors. As such, the country of Syria became a cultural mosaic, enriched by the intermingling of different belief systems, governance structures, and cultural practices. It was also eventually damned by this very diversity, today so apparent in what in some important ways became a sectarian-based civil war. Being a crossroads of history is usually great for tourism, and Syria is replete with some of the most magnificent historical and archeological landmarks in the world, but it is not necessarily good for a young country that has long been in search of a national identity.

Prior to the uprising in 2011, if you were to travel to Syria, it is likely you would have visited Palmyra (*Tadmur*) in the Syrian desert northeast of Damascus. It is an amazing place, one of the highlights of which, before it was destroyed by the Islamic State of Iraq and Syria (ISIS) in 2015, was the Temple of Baal, dedicated to a powerful pagan god emerging from several different religious traditions in the centuries before the Common Era. It was a Roman trade way station on the East–West caravan trade route (along with Petra in Jordan). While there – and a few other places in the country – a visitor would notice a number of things named "Zenobia," after the third-century CE queen who led the Palmyran kingdom in rebellion against its overlord, Rome, only to be quelled with great effort by the Roman Emperor Aurelian, personally leading his forces.

Travel almost directly west of Palmyra through Homs toward the Mediterranean coast and you will stop at the Crac de Chevaliers, the best-preserved Crusader castle in the Middle East, where the Knights Hospitallers military order attempted to protect the Christian Crusader presence in the Holy Land. So awesome is the nature of this fortress that even during the current Syrian civil war, military forces have successfully ensconced themselves inside its thick walls as protection against the destructive power of modern weaponry. Heading south to Damascus, you would likely visit the Street Called Straight, where St. Paul is said to have experienced his conversion to Christianity. A short trip northwest of Damascus and spectacularly nestled in a mountainous ravine is Maalula, a largely Christian town that is known as the last place on earth where Aramaic, the language of Jesus, is spoken. In Aleppo to the north there are churches in Christian quarters belonging to Syrian Orthodox, Syrian Catholics, Greek Orthodox, Greek Catholics, and Armenian Orthodox. To the northwest of Aleppo is the revered pilgrimage site of St. Simeon the Stylite, a Christian ascetic in the fifth century who lived on top of a pillar for decades to show his devotion to Christ. Because of this central Christian heritage, the Christian West had always expressed a particular fascination toward the area, which heightened the interest level of Europe in the region regardless of any economic or geo-strategic factors.

The rest of the country is full of historical and religious sites belonging to the dominant religion in Syria, Islam, which arrived shortly after the death of the Prophet Muhammad in the seventh century. Islam came upon a largely Judeo-Christian environment that had been under Roman/Byzantine rule. It was the minority religion in the area for some time after the Islamic conquests, especially as the Muslim conquerors showed great tolerance of existing Judeo-Christians traditions, whose practitioners were viewed as ecumenical cousins. But being a part of the religion of the political and social elite, as well as escaping a poll tax, was too seductive and led to a steady conversion that turned Syria into one of the primary bastions of Muslim power during the medieval Islamic period.

Damascus is known as one of the oldest continually inhabited cities in the world. The modern identification of Syria as an Arab and Muslim territory began in the early years of Islam in the seventh century CE. Syria was an important trading destination for Arabs in western Arabia (the Hijaz), including those in Mecca, for several centuries before the rise of Islam. The Prophet Muhammad, before he began his religious calling, apparently participated in trade caravans to Syria as a member of the Hashemite clan. The leading clan within the Quraysh tribe that dominated Mecca was known as the Abd Shams, from which emerged the Umayyad family.

The great Islamic conquests began within two years after Muhammad's passing. In keeping with his own preferences, the primary direction of conquest was toward Syria against the Byzantine empire. The Umayyad family, who apparently held extensive property in and around Damascus, played a central role in the conquest of Syria. By 638, Byzantine resistance in greater Syria had been smashed by the Muslim armies, and the second caliph or successor to the Prophet Muhammad, Umar, appointed an Umayyad as the first governor of Syria. His name was Muawiya ibn Abi Sufyan, who eventually would be primarily responsible for establishing the Umayyad caliphate based in Damascus in 661 upon the assassination of

Ali ibn Abi Talib. Over the course of its ninety years in power, there developed opposition from many different quarters in the fast-expanding Islamic world in the Middle East, North Africa, and central Asia that came under the dominion of Damascus. The expansion of Islam was a dynamic movement that, as often happens to fast-growing empires, experienced the growing pains of expansion.

The Umayyads, however, could not deliver the type of leadership that most Muslims wanted. It tended to be a regime by and for the Arabs. When the Islamic world was becoming more non-Arab and including a number of peoples who practiced religions other than Islam, this was increasingly seen as inappropriate. The ultimate result was the Abbasid revolution in 750 CE, which ended the Umayyad caliphate, shifting the center of Islam eastward to Baghdad. The Abbasids themselves, directly descended from the Prophet's family, promised a much more religiously inspired and inclusive leadership. While falling short in many ways on both these counts as the years passed, Syria receded into the background as one of a number of provinces in a growing empire. Syrians today, however, are very proud of their Umayyad past. Many distinguishing architectural gems still remain from this medieval Islamic period, such as the grand Umayyad mosque in the old city in Damascus and, most spectacularly, the Dome of the Rock in the old city of Jerusalem. Though short-lived, the Umayyad caliphate was a critically important period during the formative and oftentimes chaotic period of early Islam.

As the Abbasid empire itself began to weaken, other notable groups emerged throughout Islamic lands, including in Syria. It had become something of an accepted axiom since the days of the Pharaohs that whoever held Egypt had best control Syria as well so that it could act as something of a buffer against potential invaders from the east in addition to being an alternative bread-basket during periods of Nile flooding and subsequent famine. As such, when Abbasid power began to dissipate by the late ninth century, a succession of dynasties appeared in Egypt that more or less extended their control to Syria. First there were the Tulunids and Ikhshidids, both of whom still professed a measure of subservience to Baghdad. This was not the case with the arrival of the Fatimids in Cairo in 969 CE. The Fatimid empire became a very powerful and prosperous counterpart to the Abbasids for two centuries in the Mediterranean region. The Ayyubids of Salah al-Din al-Ayyubi (Saladin in Western chronicles) followed upon the Fatimids. Operating out of Damascus, Salah al-Din's most famous exploit came in re-capturing Jerusalem from the Crusaders in 1187.

Syria under Ottoman rule
The fairly short-lived Ayyubid dynasty was replaced by the Mamluk empire, established in Cairo in the second half of the thirteenth century and officially lasting until 1517. The Mamluks were a Turkish/Circassian

dynasty that ruled over Syria and whose architecture is still quite evident today in the country, particularly the imposing Mamluk citadel located in the heart of Aleppo. It was in 1517 that another Turkish power, the Ottomans, following upon their decisive victory against the Mamluks in 1516 at Marj Dabiq in Syria (near Aleppo), entered Cairo, thus extending their domain deep into the Middle East. Syria would become extremely important to the Ottoman sultan based in Constantinople (Istanbul), and it would be one of the few Arab territories that remained under real Ottoman control all the way up to World War I (1914–18). When the Ottoman empire expanded southward into Syria, its leaders had the good sense to recognize the diverse nature of the area based on ethnicity, religion, geography, and economic orientation in terms of trade routes. It was thus divided into semi-autonomous provinces reflective of previous orientations. Therefore, the religious and ethnic mosaic that is Syria continued unabated despite some isolated moments of sectarian conflict.

The level of autonomy in greater Syria ebbed and flowed depending upon the power of the Ottoman state. Ottoman centralization of power receded in the seventeenth and eighteenth centuries concurrent with heightened interest in Ottoman territory by a series of European powers, especially Russia. Nonetheless, Syria began to develop modern political and socio-economic institutions that sometimes reflected that which emerged in the heartland of the

Ottoman empire, but it also evolved apart from and sometimes in opposition to the dictates emanating from Constantinople. The Ottoman socio-political structure was divided vertically and horizontally in order to more efficiently rule over such an expansive multi-ethnic, multi-linguistic, and multi-religious empire. Vertically, the Ottoman government was led by the sultan and his Imperial Council, and the empire was divided into provinces (*Vilayet* or *Beylerbeyik*), which themselves were comprised of districts (*Sanjak*). What constitutes present-day Syria was essentially made up during Ottoman times of the provinces of Southern Syria, Aleppo, and Beirut. Ottoman provinces were often known – sometimes colloquially – by the name of the largest city within a parceled territory: for instance, the province officially called "Southern Syria" comprised land in current Jordan and Israel all the way south to the Gulf of Aqaba, although many in the region itself simply referred to it as "Damascus" since it was the provincial capital.

Horizontally, the Ottoman empire was divided into what was called the *millet* (nations) system. Under the millet system, in areas of religious, personal, and family law, various religious groups only had to look to their own religious authorities for adjudication. There were, *inter alia*, Greek Orthodox, Armenian Orthodox, and Jewish millets. Since Islam was officially the state religion, it was not considered a millet. It was a very tolerant type of rule, and it was also quite prudent since a large percentage of Ottoman subjects, the majority perhaps, were non-Muslim. Remnants of these vertical and horizontal divisions can still be detected today in Syria, particularly in the political and economic competition between Damascus and Aleppo that reflected the fact that the two largest cities in Syria had traditionally been competing regional centers.

As the Ottoman state continued to struggle to protect itself well into the nineteenth century, other regional powers in addition to the Europeans began to extend their influence into Syria. Muhammad Ali, the Egyptian dynast who was only nominally under Ottoman suzerainty, rebelled against his putative overlords in the early 1830s, occupying Syria for almost a decade and readying himself to move further into the Turkish heartland. It was only with European assistance that the Ottomans were able to dislodge his forces. In the aftermath of the Ottoman hiatus, however, a new class of urban notables emerged in Syria who functioned as local authorities and intermediaries with Ottoman officials. This class of notables would become important political players in Syria well into the twentieth century.

In addition, the Ottomans became subject to more pressure from the Europeans to reform the empire along the European model so it would not spontaneously collapse, which, it was feared, would generate a land-grab free-for-all that could (and eventually did) produce a pan-European conflict. In response to this pressure, the Ottomans launched the *Tanzimat* period of reform. The *Tanzimat* (regulations) officially began in 1839, but the process of modernization, or what some called defensive developmentalism, had been initiated in fits and spurts a generation earlier. While the *Tanzimat* failed to build up the strength of the empire in a manner that would enable it to defend itself against European predators, modernization – and responses to this process – occurred at a variety of levels that were felt in Syria. However, as happened in other parts of the world during the period of European imperialism, the Syrian region was brought within the orbit of European markets, ultimately to its economic disadvantage as European industries were able to produce products at a cheaper price half a world away due to mass production techniques and the economies of scale of the industrial revolution. As a result, small craft industries throughout the Middle East suffered immeasurably, which had important ramifications in terms of economic dislocation, class development, and socio-cultural norms as Syria entered the twentieth century. This bred indigenous resentment against the Europeans, of course, but also against those who could secure favorable terms of trade and/or access to European capital, mostly minority Christian and Jewish groups.

There were different responses to continued European encroachment and modernization efforts in the Middle East. Through the proliferation of newspapers and book publishing, not only were new scientific, financial, and even philosophical ideas disseminated from the West, but so too were important socio-political ideologies. Among them were the rise of liberal constitutionalism, the development of a nascent form of Arab nationalism or proto-nationalism, and the emergence of pan-Islamism. Syria became one of the foci of the proto-Arab nationalist response, engendered by a combination of factors, including, *inter alia*: the rediscovery and new appreciation of Arab heritage and the role the Arabs played in the founding and establishment of Islam, which was bound so tightly with the emergence of the pan-Islamic Salafiyya movement in the late nineteenth century; the so-called "Arab awakening" spurred on by an Arab literary movement – and greater availability of printing presses – centered in the Levant in the second half of the 1800s; and, finally, the ever-tightening control of the Ottomans, especially as European penetration into the Balkans and Middle East continued unabated, while Syria remained one of the few areas to remain under Ottoman rule.

What is interesting is that despite the centralization policy emanating from Constantinople, Arab nationalists in Syria tended to agitate for more autonomy rather than outright independence from the Ottoman empire. This general feeling lasted all the way into World War I. For better or worse, the Ottoman structure had become something of the accepted status quo not easily abandoned. The Arab Muslim majority in Syria, already resentful of the socio-economic benefits the minority Christians in the area received from European powers, avidly supported the pan-Islamism espoused by Ottoman Sultan Abd al-Hamid II. In return for this support, the Ottomans continued to assist in the development of Syria's agricultural and commercial sectors, mutually reinforcing the long-standing links developed between Constantinople and cities in Syria, thus bolstering the development of a landed elite who became local power brokers and whose influence continued long after the Ottomans receded from the area. However, the authoritarian and repressive policies in Syria of the Young Turk government that came to power in 1908, combined with the depredations of World War I, including military conscription, higher taxes, and confiscation of livestock and other resources, turned more Syrians against the Ottomans, and they began to entertain the idea of separation from the empire. As elsewhere in the region, the war was a significant turning point for what would become the modern nation-state system in the Middle East.

2

World War I

World War I is the most important period in the history of the modern Middle East. This is certainly the case for what would become modern Syria. Many, if not most, of the important issues in the Middle East during the twentieth century and into the twenty-first century, such as Arab nationalism, Arab nation-state formation and the question of identity, Islamic extremism, the Arab–Israeli conflict, and even the conflicts in the Persian Gulf region since 1980, can be traced to the events that transpired in the region during and immediately after the "war to end all wars." Although the epicenter of the conflict was always in Europe, and events in the Middle East were always of secondary concern to the course of the war on the continent for the primary European combatants, nonetheless, to the countries and peoples of the region, it had a direct and long-lasting effect.

For the Middle East, World War I was a tremendously complex period, comprised of the establishment of new states, the end of the Ottoman empire, the evincing of nationalist and territorial goals on the part of Arabs and Zionists, and the intervention of European powers with crisscrossing, ambiguous, changing, and often contradictory promises, pledges, and declarations. As such, for the relatively uniniti-ated, this is also a period in modern Middle Eastern history that is quite difficult to comprehend. It has been my experience that the most efficient way to understand its complexities is first and foremost to examine the British role. Britain was, by far, the prime mover of events in the Middle East during and immediately after the war. It was London that had the most influence in the region of all of the European powers before, during, and after the conflagration. It was London that largely initiated and engaged in the diplomatic machinations that resulted in such infa-mous documents as the Sykes–Picot Agreement, the Hussein–McMahon correspondence, and the Balfour Declaration, each of which will be discussed shortly, not to even mention the postwar negotiations that led to the redrawing of the map in the Middle East, including Syria, that has essentially remained geo-graphically static since that time.

For Britain, the decision by the Ottomans to enter the war on the side of the German-led Central powers instantly transformed its age-old policy toward the Ottoman empire. For over a century it had been British policy to maintain the integrity of that empire so as to ensure the lifeline to India and create a buffer to Russian expansionist designs toward the heart-land of the Middle East. Although to many this stated policy may have seemed more like lip service when set against Britain's actions in terms of its own terri-torial control over Ottoman lands and interference in

Ottoman affairs, now the Ottomans were the enemy, and their defeat became official policy. As such, the Middle East was fair game, and Syria would play a pivotal role in the unfolding drama.

Plans began to emerge early in the war regarding the disposition of Ottoman territories, particularly those regions in the Middle East that were still under Ottoman control, such as Syria, Palestine, and Iraq. In the immediate sense, once hostilities commenced in the war, British policy in the Middle East revolved around the following: (1) the strategic necessity of defeating the Ottoman empire; (2) the creation of a pro-British bulwark in the Arab territories of the empire that most believed would be detached from Constantinople (Istanbul) in some form or fashion; and (3) accomplishing both of these objectives while not upsetting London's allies, France and Russia, especially as they were bearing the brunt of the German offensives. This was a tall task, and in order to achieve its goals in the Middle East, Britain expediently constructed, amended, and reversed its policies depending upon the exigencies of the diplomatic and military situation at any given moment, producing in the end what on the surface seemed to be contradictory pledges to a variety of states and groups as well as setting up unrealistic parameters for success in the region that would in many ways shape the course of modern Middle Eastern history.

The war in Europe had clearly drawn to a virtual stalemate by 1915, characterized by static trench warfare. The British war cabinet argued for opening up another front in southeastern Europe. To do this, however, first necessitated a military confrontation with the Ottomans. Thus what would become the British-led Gallipoli campaign, beginning in February 1915, was intended to swiftly knock the Ottomans out of the war. It turned out to be a disaster. The ultimate failure at Gallipoli, which became apparent by the fall of 1915, compelled the British to seek an alternative route toward defeating the Ottomans in the Middle East, a path that would ultimately lead to a campaign directed by General Sir Edmund Allenby emanating out of Egypt up through Palestine toward Damascus. Not by design did Syria become an integral part of World War I. The failure also forced Britain to recognize that it might need some assistance not only in this task but also in the postwar strategic map in the region, which would lead various British representatives to negotiate with groups of Arabs and Zionists competing to convince London that they could serve its interests better than anyone else.

British and French Negotiations

France, for its part, was becoming a bit concerned that while it was bearing the brunt of the war on the western front, Britain was in the process of stealing away with the Middle East. The British, however, began to listen more intently to French concerns by late 1915, when it became clear that the Gallipoli campaign had failed.

The British, therefore, would not be able to impose at will their designs on the Middle East. The diplomatic battleground in the region between the two European powers would revolve around Syria, including present-day Israel/Palestine and Lebanon. The French believed that Syria was practically its birthright, and France also had a direct interest in the disposition of the Ottoman empire, as it provided forty-five percent of the private sector foreign capital in the empire and assumed sixty percent of the Ottoman public debt.[1]

There were some practical reasons beyond Gallipoli that compelled the British to make concessions to the French. If the British were to continue to militarily engage the Ottoman empire, they would have to divert resources from the western front, something that would require French acquiescence, and Paris would only do so for a price – British negotiator Sir Mark Sykes understood this. In addition, another plan was being hatched to aid the British cause in the Middle East, one involving a possible Arab revolt led by the Sharif Hussein (Hussein ibn Ali al-Hashimi), the leader in the Hijaz and Guardian of the Two Holy Places (Mecca and Medina). So, concurrently with negotiations with representatives of the sharif, the British hastened to meet with French diplomats to find mutual accord so that plans could move forward in the region.

The French sent François Georges Picot as their representative, and negotiations began in November 1915. What came to be called the Sykes–Picot

Agreement was consummated in May 1916, and consisted of dividing the heartland of the Arab world
into spheres of influence. The French could assume
direct control over the coast of Syria west of a line
running north–south from Aleppo through Hama and
Homs to Damascus (including modern-day Lebanon,
which, at the time, consisted of a large and economically important Arab Christian population that had
long had ties with France), while the interior of Syria
would be a "sphere of influence" subject to some level
of indirect control. The French also received the province of Mosul within their sphere of influence in what
is now northern Iraq, while the British would retain
the Ottoman provinces of Baghdad and Basra to the
south down to the Persian Gulf. From the British perspective, this would not only allay French concerns,
but it would also construct a French buffer between
Russia and British-controlled territories in the Middle
East. Palestine was a different story, however: both
Britain and France wanted it within their respective
spheres of influence. What was finally agreed to more
for the sake of expediency than anything else was
that neither the British nor the French would receive
Palestine; instead, most of the territory, including
Jerusalem, would fall under some sort of international
administration that would be delineated by an unde-
termined mechanism following the war. The extent to
which most British officials actually thought of Arab
independence as a reality is a different question, since
many viewed the Arabs as incapable of statehood in

the short term and as a vehicle through which Britain could exert its influence in the region. In addition, the British believed that it would just be a matter of time before they were able to establish facts on the ground through military action in order to secure Palestine.

Arab Involvement and the Sharifian Revolt

The Sharif Hussein was a Hashemite and therefore a direct descendant of the family of the Prophet Muhammad. He was, as noted above, the Guardian of the Two Holy Places in the Hijaz region of Arabia. He was also an opportunist who had come to the conclusion that he needed a patron in order to realize his territorial ambitions. It was under these circumstances that he began his first halting steps toward establishing a relationship with the British.

One of the sharif's sons, Faisal, stopped in the hotbed of nascent Arab nationalism in Damascus in March 1915 on his way to Constantinople. There he met with representatives of Arab secret societies such as al-'Ahd and al-Fatat, who were bent on at least obtaining more autonomy from Ottoman rule, to discuss the possibilities of drawing up a program of action and cooperation with the Hijazis. While Faisal was in the Ottoman capital, members of the secret societies drew up what came to be called the Damascus Protocol, which outlined Arab demands to the British in return for rebelling against the Turks. It essentially called for British recognition of Arab independence in Syria (including present-day Lebanon, Israel, and Jordan), Iraq, and Arabia.[2] Faisal brought the Damascus Protocol to his father, whereupon it was adopted as the basis for Hashemite policy with the British. A number of leading members of the secret societies in Damascus, though certainly not all, agreed to accept Hussein as the Arab leader of any movement that might develop. Although still tentative regarding the British, it was under such conditions, armed with the apparent means to deliver a real rebellion, that the sharif initiated what came to be known as the Hussein–McMahon correspondence.

Sir Henry McMahon, the British high commissioner in Egypt, received sanction from London to negotiate with Hussein an Arab revolt. A letter from McMahon dated October 24, 1915, was sent to the sharif. In it the high commissioner, in return for a sharifian-led Arab revolt, offered independence to the Arabs along the lines of the Damascus Protocol, with three reservations: that is, it did not specify the borders of an independent Arab state but qualified a nebulous offer with restrictions. The Arabs would gain independence except in areas: (1) which the British decided were not "purely Arab," which meant the eastern Mediterranean coast, or west of the line in Syria that goes from Aleppo in the north through Hama, Homs, and then Damascus in the south; (2) in which the special interests of France limited Britain – this pertained especially to the interior of Syria east of the aforementioned line as delineated in Sykes–Picot; and (3)

in which Britain had already existing treaties, referring primarily to longstanding agreements between
London and the Persian Gulf Arab shaykhdoms.

The first two reservations would cause most of the
consternation and bitter debate that has ensued ever
since regarding what actually was included in an independent Arab state that might emerge out of the war.
The different interpretations surrounding the first res-
ervation would become particularly relevant with the
onset of the Arab–Israeli conflict because it dealt with
the disposition of Palestine. The reference to French
interests has also come under intense scrutiny, especially in relation to the eighteen-month Arab kingdom
in Syria headed by Faisal following the war that for-
cibly gave way to French control. It seems as though
Hussein was aware of British concern for French
interests, as was made clear to him in McMahon's final
letter in the correspondence of January 1916, but it is
unclear how much the sharif knew (or was told) the
extent to which they were being met.

The Arab revolt launched by Faisal in June 1916
and assisted by the British liaison officer T. E.
Lawrence came and went, yet no specific border discussions ensued during the war. McMahon's language
in his letters has been variously described as flowery
and ambiguous, and purposely so since he knew of
the simultaneous negotiations with the French over
much of the same land. In strict diplomatic language,
certainly in keeping with accepted Western standards
of the day, there was no legal contradiction since there

was no official document to stand up to Sykes–Picot, which itself did not survive the war unscathed and unaltered. And certainly the British were quite adept at always making sure, as good diplomats do, that there was an "out" if necessary regarding specific and legal commitments – something the Zionists would find out for themselves a few years after the 1917 Balfour Declaration declaring Britain's support for a "national home for the Jewish people" in Palestine.

It became politically desirable for the British to trumpet the Arab role in the campaign in order to secure pro-British allies in the interior of Syria in the hopes of warding off the French by rewriting Sykes–Picot with facts on the ground. A number of leading Arabs in Syria essentially disavowed Hashemite claims, marking the beginning of a process that would become manifest in the postwar years; indeed, the British themselves became progressively disenchanted with Hussein, viewing him as a bombastic, self-aggrandized would-be dynast, and they increasingly turned to a rising force led by Abd al-Aziz ibn Abd al-Rahman Al Saud in Arabia, allowing the latter to effectively jettison Hussein into exile soon after the war. From the British perspective, since the sharif did not deliver a revolt of the magnitude that they were led to believe, then any promises made to the Arabs, whether implicit or explicit, were essentially null and void – they did not deliver, so they did not necessarily deserve even what was inferred in the Hussein–McMahon   correspondence.   Only   self-interest militated against further extortion with continued British support of the Arab cause in Syria for a brief time during the Faisali period.

End of the War and Postwar Negotiations

By the end of 1917, following the Bolshevik revolution, not only had the new Soviet regime withdrawn from the conflict, but also, to the embarrassment of Russia's erstwhile Entente allies, it soon thereafter published the secret wartime agreements, most damaging of which was Sykes–Picot. The apparent contradictions in the various pledges from Britain started to become manifest, but with approximately one million troops on the ground in the Middle Eastern theater by war's end, the British appeared not to care. General Allenby's Palestine campaign had taken Jerusalem by December 1917 and Damascus, Beirut, and Aleppo by October 1918.

It was during this time that the various political ramifications of the division of the Arab lands of the Ottoman empire became of immediate concern. The taking of Damascus became enmeshed in postwar diplomacy before the fighting was even over. Just how much should the British honor French interests as articulated in Sykes–Picot? Just how much should the British honor an apparent pledge to the Arabs as articulated in the Hussein–McMahon correspondence, and could this be an indirect way to keep the French boxed in along the Syrian coast rather than allow them to extend their influence into the interior of Syria? How much could the British dictate and, if necessary, reshape the terms of the postwar order in the Middle East with troops abounding across the region? And how would the commitment to the Zionists made in the Balfour Declaration fit into the mix? These were among the myriad of questions facing the British in the last year of the war and into the postwar diplomatic environment.

By early 1918 the British had moved away from Hussein. If anything, British officials attempted to build up Faisal as a viable alternative, to the distress of his father, who claimed the British were manipulating his son against him. The Declaration to the Seven made in June 1918, which was an attempt by the British to shore up their position with the Arabs and reinforce their commitment to Arab independence with seven Arab nationalist representatives from Syria, clearly indicates an attempt to find an alternative to Hussein.

The British had actually been negotiating with Syrian Arabs in Cairo since early 1918 in an attempt to find an accommodation with the Balfour Declaration. The most assertive attempt to do so at this time was the creation of a Zionist commission led by Chaim Weizmann, who was the leading Zionist in Britain, the architect of Balfour, and, later, the first president of Israel. The commission was sent to Palestine, where Weizmann met with Prince Faisal, who was apparently willing to accommodate Zionist aspirations in

Palestine in return for British support for his own aspirations in Syria. This accordance between Faisal and Weizmann would lead to Faisal's tacit support for the Zionist program at the Paris peace conference a year later in 1919. Regardless of the specious nature of Faisal having any authority to speak for Palestinian Arabs, it is interesting to posit that the later betrayal of Faisal by the British to satisfy French interests in Syria may not only have antagonized British–Arab relations that much more, but also may have sounded the death-knell for the last possibility that Zionism could be accepted in Palestine by at least one important Arab entity.

The British, however, were attempting, as Sykes stated in 1917, to combine "Meccan Patriarchalism with Syrian Urban intelligentsia."[3] This was, in essence, the intent of the Declaration to the Seven. It declared as independent lands already under control of the Arabs and those lands liberated by the Arabs, while those areas under Entente control would be subject to negotiation. This opened the door ever so slightly for the sharifian army, if the "conquest" of Syria could be arranged for them by the British. Faisal was the least objectionable of the Hijazis to the Syrians, especially since the latter began to realize that independence could not come without the former. In this way, Sykes could maintain some semblance of Hussein–McMahon while those British officials who had utter disdain for the concessions made to the French could utilize the Arabs to prevent Paris from extending its control beyond the Syrian coast. Indeed, as is well known, Faisal's forces were allowed to enter Damascus first by the British, even though the Turks had long evacuated the city in anticipation of Allenby's advance to the north from Palestine. It was important that Arab forces entered Damascus first, therefore ameliorating French concerns that the British intended to take Syria while at the same time placing someone in Damascus through whom the British could extend their influence while keeping the French effectively locked up on the coast. These first months of Arab "rule" in Damascus were quite chaotic amidst British and French machinations to secure the interior of Syria through Arab surrogates.

Despite French efforts, British policy had a friend in this regard in Paris. French President Georges Clemenceau was about as disinclined to extend French foreign commitments as British Prime Minister David Lloyd George was inclined to maintain them. On December 1, 1918, Lloyd George met with Clemenceau in London, and the British prime minister basically got what he wanted in a verbal agreement. Clemenceau gave him Mosul, an oil-rich Ottoman province in northern present-day Iraq, which had been previously ceded to the French under Sykes–Picot, and the French president acquiesced to British control of Palestine as a trade-off to secure control over Syria.

It was under these circumstances that the victorious powers met in Paris in January 1919 to begin to discuss the postwar environment. It was a venue in which US President Woodrow Wilson made a celebrated, albeit brief, intervention into the maelstrom of international diplomacy, dominating the direction of negotiations on the surface due to US economic power and new-found military strength. But Wilson was inexperienced, if not naïve, in the ways of European diplomacy. Nowhere was this more apparent than in what became known as the King–Crane Commission. Wilson's intent was to help resolve potential British and French differences over the disposition of the Arab territories of the Ottoman empire by sending a commission to the region itself in order to ascertain the desires of the indigenous populations.

Henry Churchill King, president of Oberlin College, and Charles R. Crane, a businessman from Chicago and a Democratic Party activist, led a group of Americans to Palestine, Syria, Lebanon, and Anatolia in the summer of 1919. In Syria, the commission found that public opinion there preferred no mandate (and no separation of Syria and Palestine), but if a mandate was to be imposed on them, then the preference was that it would first be supervised by the United States, or, failing that, Britain – by no means was there any indication of desire for a French mandate. The King–Crane Commission report, even in the best of circumstances, would be non-binding – it was simply informational in an attempt to shore up Wilson's position. But we know that Lloyd George and Clemenceau, while paying lip service to Wilson's

tactics, had already gone a long way toward decid-
ing who was going to get what in the Middle East,
the French still holding out for their interpretation
of some measure of supervision over the interior of
Syria. The commission report was, in the end, essentially ignored by the Europeans.

At the peace conference, Clemenceau would doggedly try to at least acquire the measure of supervision
over the interior of Syria that had been mentioned
in Sykes–Picot. Faisal also attended the conference,
and he just as doggedly tried to hold on to Syria. The
French were not assuaged by Britain's support for Arab
independence since they knew Faisal was beholden to
the British financially, politically, and militarily. Syria
was essentially the only bone of contention left to be
negotiated out of the rump of the Ottoman empire.
The problem is that even though many of the Arab
provinces of the Ottoman empire had already been
allotted, final and official acknowledgement of such
was the last element of the overall postwar negotiations to be settled; of course, this was especially the
case in Syria. As such, events regionally and internationally began to negatively affect Britain's ability to
achieve its initial objectives.

The regional and international environments were
quite different by the fall of 1919 and into 1920 than
they were in 1916 and 1917. Russia had withdrawn
from the war and the specter of Bolshevism cast a
shadow over the Paris negotiations. The United States
had begun to adopt a more isolationist posture that

would come to characterize its interwar diplomacy, especially as Wilson suffered a debilitating stroke in September 1919, thus removing the internationalist wing's most vocal and influential advocate. Congress did not ratify the Treaty of Versailles, which brought the war to an end, nor US participation in the League of Nations. Britain itself, as economic problems mounted and the military remained overextended, would be forced into retrenchment mode in the Middle East, thus reducing its bargaining leverage. Together these were compelling reasons for Lloyd George to make concessions to France regarding Syria. He could no longer count on the United States to play an active role in Europe and contain Germany – now he realized he had to rely more on the French for balance-of-power politics on the continent; indeed, the British prime minister would tellingly comment that "France is worth ten Syrias." In addition, his colleague in Paris fell from office in January 1920. Alexandre Millerand became the new French president, and he was someone who was much less inclined to make any concessions on Syria as well as more inclined to take advantage of Britain's decreasing leverage in the area.

It was these conditions that compelled the British to announce in September 1919 that they would withdraw their troops from the Syrian region, thus leaving Faisal to fend for himself against the French. With the British out of the way in Syria, Paris and London could finally close the diplomatic book with regard to the disposition of the Ottoman empire. So in April

1920 at San Remo, Italy, the Entente powers apportioned the Arab world between Britain and France,
assigning mandates that would later be formalized
by the League of Nations in September 1922. Britain
obtained Palestine (including present-day Jordan) and
Mesopotamia (Iraq), and its status in Egypt and in the
Persian Gulf was confirmed. The French were assigned
the Syrian mandate, including Lebanon. The term
"mandate" was another bone thrown to Wilsonian
sensitivities regarding imperialism. In other words,
these were not protectorates or colonies in the Middle
East; they were supposed to be more like international
trusteeships. The mandates were to be supervised by
the mandatory powers, ostensibly preparing them
for eventual independence, although the mandatory
powers were not particularly interested in this.

By the summer of 1920, then, Faisal was living on
borrowed time in Syria. The French, after quickly dis-
patching armed resistance outside of Damascus with
their force of some ninety thousand troops, ended
the brief Hashemite kingdom of Syria in July 1920,
taking direct charge of what would become their
Syrian mandate. Faisal's withdrawal from Syria had
important repercussions for Palestine. Up until that
time, a number of Palestinians worked in high-level
positions in Faisal's administration, and for the most
part, Palestinians in general supported a greater Syria
under Faisal's rule, one obviously that would include
Palestine. Faisal seemed to be the horse on which to
ride toward at least some semblance of independence.

As evidence of this, the first two Palestinian national congresses were held in Damascus; the third, however, after Faisal's expulsion, was held in Haifa in December 1920. In retrospect, the British abandonment of Faisal in Syria may have had repercussions far beyond the issue of betraying Arab interests to the French.

The British were unable to keep the French bottled up along the Syrian coast, but they certainly did not want French influence to extend beyond Syria itself. In order to meet this potential strategic threat at a time of British retrenchment in the region, it was decided at a conference in Cairo in March 1921, attended by Winston Churchill and T. E. Lawrence and dealing primarily with Transjordan (later Jordan) and Iraq, to make Abdullah (Hussein's third son and the great-great-grandfather of the current King Abdullah of Jordan) the sovereign of Transjordan. Since Abdullah at that very moment had entered Amman with the apparent intent of liberating Syria for his brother, Faisal, it seemed like the proper thing to do in order to ward off a potential conflict with the French that could draw the British in. Abdullah was officially recognized as Emir of Transjordan by the British in December 1921. In this way, as the British typically did, London could work through a surrogate beholden to British interests and reliant upon British force to maintain its influence in the region, keep the French out, and hopefully assuage the Arabs. For good measure, and as much an attempt at restitution as strategic motivation, at the conference it was agreed that Faisal would be made the king of the newly stitched-to-gether entity now called Iraq, supported by a number of former Arab nationalist Ottoman officers who had been with him in Damascus. He officially assumed his new position in August 1921. As for Syria, it formally entered the period of the French mandate.

3

The French Mandate

In April 1920 at San Remo, Italy, the mandate system officially apportioned the Middle Eastern territories of the defeated Ottoman empire between Britain and France. While Britain's position in Iraq and Egypt was confirmed, it was also awarded Palestine and Transjordan as mandated territories. France, on the other hand, received Syria and Lebanon. Although the borders in some areas were still murky and would be tweaked as time went on, the modern nation-state system in the heartland of the Middle East was coming into existence. Of course, in Syria there was still the little matter of the existing Hashemite kingdom under Faisal bin Hussein. This would not in the least deter the French, especially, as pointed out in the previous chapter, when the British decided to not obstruct them in Syria. A French armed contingent was dispatched from Beirut toward Damascus in July 1920, and after what is certainly seen in Syrian history as a heroic struggle of national martyrdom at the Battle of Maysaloun outside of the capital, an outmanned and outgunned Syrian army was decisively defeated. The French moved into Damascus and began to organize their mandate. The League of Nations officially approved of the French mandate in Syria two years later in 1922.

French interests in Syria had been longstanding. This was certainly the view among sections of the French foreign policy elite in Paris, composed of hardcore colonialists and French Catholics. Maintaining French influence in the Holy Land was a foreign policy priority in the period before, during, and especially after World War I, even though the French population as a whole was not particularly keen on the idea amid postwar economic challenges. The colonial lobby in France had mainly strategic and economic interests in the eastern Mediterranean. Certainly after the opening of the Suez Canal in 1869, funded and built by British and French companies, as well as the alarming (from the point of view of Paris) presence of Britain in Egypt by 1882 as well as in the Persian Gulf and in Mesopotamia, gaining a foothold in the Levant was important. Along with the enduring French presence in North Africa, a sphere of influence, if not colonial presence, in Syria was seen as something of a strategic necessity. It is important to remember that even though Britain and France were allied during World War I, Paris and London each saw the other as a potential rival, if not enemy, following the conflict, picking up on their intense colonial competition prior to the war.

In addition, France had invested more by far in the Ottoman empire than had any other European power since the late nineteenth century – more than double that of Germany by the eve of the Great War in 1914. This was especially the case in greater Syria, where French companies built the port of Beirut and invested in and built most of the country's railroads, including a line connecting Beirut with Damascus and the Hawran in the southwestern quadrant of the country. French companies were also heavily invested in a variety of other industries in Ottoman territories in the Middle East, from tobacco to public utilities. The economic investment and development in Syria and Lebanon was heavily concentrated along the coastal areas, and in particular among minority communities (Christian Maronites in Lebanon), who related to and often spoke the languages of their European investors. This gave these minority groups an economic advantage long resented by the majority Sunni Muslim community in a way that became reflected in political divisions as well. Indeed, French Catholics often saw France – and themselves – as protectors of Christian communities in the Levant, much as Czarist Russia saw itself as the natural protector of Greek Orthodox Christians in the Middle East. It was both sincere and used as a wedge to enter into Middle Eastern politics and extend French influence in the region. This just reinforced the French perception that the Christian communities in the Arab world were more progressive and enlightened while the Muslim majority tended to be backward looking and fanatical. This sectarian view of Syria would persist during the mandate years and consistently hamper a cogent diagnosis of the more nuanced problems that would arise during the French occupation. In the end, however, there was a general feeling in France's policymaking circles that acquiring and maintaining its position in the Levant was a matter of great-power prestige.

The mandate system structure itself was somewhat confusing to the French. The mandatory power was supposed to guide the mandated territory and population toward eventual independence. From the beginning, however, the French, despite some constraints placed on them by the League of Nations Mandate Commission, which had really no enforceable capacity, viewed their presence in Syria and Lebanon as nothing short of traditional colonialism; indeed, French policy in Morocco was seen as a guide for its policies in Syria.

In fact, as Philip Khoury pointed out in his magisterial book *Syria and the French Mandate: The Politics of Arab Nationalism, 1920–1945*, there was a great deal of continuity in the nature of rule by an outside power from the Ottomans to the French, particularly in the make-up of the traditional landowning Syrian families who had acted for decades as the interlocutors, thus the local power brokers, between the Ottoman authorities and the population as a whole. This paradigm essentially continued on uninterrupted when the French came, except for one very important difference: the French has little to no legitimacy. It mattered not whether the metropole of power was in Constantinople/Istanbul or Paris – both were seen as distant by Syrians – but at least the Ottomans shared a religion and a history with the largely Syrian Arab community, and the Ottoman Sublime Porte had several centuries of legitimacy as overlord of the region, something the French did not share. Indeed, as stated earlier, France reinforced its otherness by having established close ties with and promoting minority communities in greater Syria. So the French came into Syria with little tailwind and considerable headwind, and then engaged in policies that only exacerbated the situation during the mandate. As Khoury wrote,

> The advent of French rule in Syria did not fundamentally change the behavior patterns of urban leaders or the fundamental character of political life. But there was a significant difference in the nature of the new imperial authority: it was illegitimate and thus was unstable. France was not recognized to be a legitimate overlord, as the Sultan-Caliph of the Ottoman Empire had been.[1]

The socio-economically debilitating and dislocating effects of the war in Syria only made the job of the French that much tougher.

The artificiality of the postwar settlement in the heartland of the Middle East, geographically and demographically, severed traditional Syrian links to other areas. Arbitrary borders were drawn between Syria and its neighbors, in each case separating populations from what had been their traditional socio-cultural and economic connections. Damascus looked toward and traded with Jerusalem and Baghdad more than the other major city in the new Syria, Aleppo. However, Jerusalem and Baghdad were now located in British mandate territory, Palestine and Iraq, respectively, and therefore much less accessible. The same with Aleppo, where its traditional orientation was toward cities in Turkey and toward Mosul – the latter also now located in the British mandate of Iraq – not toward Damascus. Arabs were "caught" on the Turkish side of the new border, and many Turkish speakers now found themselves in an Arab-dominated state. And Kurds, Syriac Christians, and Armenians, among others, found themselves on both sides of a border, brewing a combustible recipe for ethnic tension that for decades would sporadically boil over – one example of which is the current Syrian civil war. Arab tribes along the new Syrian–Iraqi border, who had freely migrated back and forth in the region, were in many cases split apart. An already complex mosaic of religious and ethnic diversity in Syria was thus complicated that much more by new international boundaries. It is little wonder that the question of identity would become a central issue in the evolution of the Syrian nation-state.

Divide and Rule

The external partitioning imposed by the victorious European powers was not the only thing that disoriented the Syrian population. Internal divisions as well caused dislocation and socio-economic hardships.

With the opposition of the majority Sunni Muslim population in Syria to French rule, mandatory authorities adopted a policy of "divide and rule" tactics first honed in colonial Morocco. In this sense the French could utilize the fissiparous ethnic and religious nature of Syria against itself in order to prevent any coherent opposition from forming. The Maronite Christians in Lebanon had been the most pro-French element among the various sects; therefore, the French expanded the border of the Ottoman district of Mount Lebanon and administered the area as a separate entity, which ultimately became the core of modern Lebanon. The remainder of French-mandated Syria was then divided into five zones. Each division was chosen to play upon traditional rivalries. Latakia was carved out for the Alawites, Alexandretta for the Turks, and Jabal al-Druze (Suwayda) for the Druze. The Sunni Muslims were divided between Aleppo and Damascus. In this way, not only did extended families, especially the richer landowning ones, have to cope with land holdings and other economic interests that now crossed new international borders and were governed by different national administrative and tax systems, but also inside Syria, socio-economic mobility was disrupted by the cantons created by the French. It wasn't until 1936 that attempts were made to administratively unify the semi-autonomous zones, and not until World War II that it actually happened.

Moreover, the Alawites were brought into the local military force in numbers far exceeding their share of the population. For the traditionally persecuted Alawite sect, joining the military, looked upon with derision by most other Syrians because of the tacit cooperation with the French, was one of their few avenues for upward social mobility. It turned out to be quite serendipitous following World War II when the military became politicized and used as a political instrument for acquiring power; the Alawites were then in an advantageous position to advance within the political system, eventually dominating the military-security apparatus and, thus, political power by the mid-1960s. The Sunni Arab nationalists, on the other hand, as primarily members of the urban educated classes, were isolated from much of the country during the mandate years. As such, French rule was generally regarded by Syrians as oppressive. French authorities, in the aftermath of the economic drain of World War I and faced with an increasingly hostile indigenous population, spent over one-third of Syria's tax revenues on public security. As Khoury points out, four billion of the five billion francs that France invested in Syria during the mandate period went toward defense, with only the remaining billion being invested in the economy and infrastructure.[2]

There was also cultural imperialism. French was introduced in schools at the expense of Arabic. Singing the French national anthem was required and the Syrian pound was pegged to the French franc, which became legal tender. French architecture, still recognizable in the main cities of Syria today, was introduced in everything from street patterns to building design. Embittered Syrian nationalists played upon these obvious symbols of the French presence and won widespread support in their opposition to French rule. And French mandate policy was anything but consistent. Domestic politics in France were quite volatile in the interwar period, and governments shifted back and forth between the political left and right, mostly based on domestic economic issues and European affairs. If the French left on the political spectrum tended to want to draw down on empire and therefore had a willingness to make concessions and grant more autonomy in Syria, if not a clear path toward independence, the political right was almost the exact opposite, wanting to maintain, even enhance, France's presence in its colonial territories for strategic reasons. But in the end it often simply came down to national prestige – maintaining the growing fiction of being a great power. These frequent shifts in French policy were confusing to Syrian national politicians, oftentimes offering the hope of true independence only to have it dashed by the fall of a government in Paris and the rise of a new one that was decidedly less ameliorating.

The overall policy of the French mandate fueled the development of an amorphous nationalism in Syria. I say "amorphous" because there developed over the course of the mandate two nationalisms in Syria, that of Syrian nationalism, beholden to the greater glory of the Syrian nation-state (and for most, the reconstitution of greater Syria), as well as that of Arab national-ism, the percolating idea that the Arabs should have a nation-state of their own across the region where Arab ethno-linguistic traits are dominant. These two devel-oping nationalist visions certainly saw the French as an unwelcome interloper, and they therefore cooper-ated on many occasions, but they also in many ways competed against each other, a trend that would become more overt in the 1950s after independence.

But these were not the only ideological reactions to the mandate system. In what tended to be the case across the Middle East, there were three general responses to the mandate period – among those who cared to notice and take action. First and foremost was the nationalist response, which tended to be secular and promoted by those who had had some contact with Western education and ideas. They had been educated in modern, secular professional schools and had acquired administrative experience in the Ottoman system and in the short-lived polity of King Faisal.[3] They also learned to operate outside of the mainstream in secret societies in places such as Damascus, Cairo, Jerusalem, and Beirut before and during the war. As it was primarily a secular move-ment, its leadership was composed of important Christian and Muslim Arabs.

Secondly, there was an Islamist response. Smaller in numbers and political influence at first, the embodi-ment of this reaction was the founding of the Muslim Brotherhood by Hassan al-Banna in 1928 in Egypt, a country that was subject to British control, influence, and political manipulation. A Syrian branch of the Muslim Brotherhood would eventually form. This was not a surprise considering the Muslim Brotherhood was (and continues to be) a Sunni Islamist movement. It thus naturally appealed to a majority Sunni population in Syria that felt increasingly marginalized by French tactics. Traditional Sunni elements in Syria would continue to feel marginalized, isolated, and repressed under successive secular political movements that came to power in the country, culminating with the rise of the socialist Baath Party in the early 1960s. This feeling of marginalization and disempowerment would, as we shall see later in the book, burst out into open rebellion in the late 1970s and early 1980s and then again in 2011.

The third general response across the region was a fascist one, which in Syria actually tended to find some receptivity with the Syrian nationalists in terms of the glorification of the state. Fascist movements in the Middle East, as elsewhere in the world, were delegitimized by the horrors of Nazism in Germany before and during World War II, and they therefore disappeared from the region fairly quickly. Syrian nationalists survived this, and became identified with the SSNP (Syrian Social Nationalist Party), which, like the Baathists, would play a more important role after independence.

The nationalists in Syria, however, comprised but a small portion of the population in the Syrian mandate. Their leadership, as C. Ernest Dawn noted, tended to be the same class of intermediaries with whom the Ottoman administration worked in order to more effectively extend their local rule in the area.[4] Increasingly, by the late nineteenth century, as the result of the new land and private property made available and the commercial laws and practices promulgated under the *Tanzimat* reforms, the leading families in Syria were landowners and merchants rather than religious shaykhs or descendants of princely figures of the past. These became the local power brokers. The crackdown, repressions, and executions by the Ottomans during World War I accelerated the transition of Syrian activists from advocating a kind of proto-Arab nationalism into a full-fledged one after the war, calling for outright independence.

Interestingly, French officials made contact with and encouraged some of the Arab nationalist secret societies in Syria operating under the noses of the Ottomans in order to help undermine Ottoman rule during the war. The relationship went nowhere, and, indeed, Syrian Arab nationalists felt abandoned by the French when the latter's economic and strategic interests militated against closer cooperation. So, the inevitable opposition of Arab nationalists to the French slipped into the mandate period with a tailwind of distrust and recrimination. But owing to the exigencies of shifting overlords from the Ottomans to the French, the landowning elite, many of whom were urban notables who for decades had to get along with the Ottomans in order to maintain their socio-economic status, now, perforce, were to become Arabists, that is, Arab nationalists – and they had to deal with the French. They were compelled to play this role, but they became ultimately enmeshed in a self-defeating dialectic: the population increasingly wanted the French out and true independence, and the urban notables would agitate for them both, but only to a certain point. Since their status and wealth depended on the system at hand, they became consciously and unconsciously co-opted by the French into keeping it. And as stated earlier, from time to time there would be French ruling coalitions in Paris that made Syrian independence seem like something that would happen in the near rather than long term. It was a delicate balancing act.

Urban notables, intellectuals, and professionals, raised on the Western-inspired notions of parliamentary systems and constitutions, and buoyed by the heritage of constitutional movements in the Ottoman empire on two separate occasions as well as the imposition of French political life, worked for independence within the French-imposed parliamentary system in Syria. However, there was a younger generation of Syrians, many of whom were reading Marx and Engels (or the Quran for Islamists) rather than the writings of Locke, Voltaire, and Mill that inspired their parents' generation. This younger generation became politically aware and active under the mandate system itself. They could be patient no longer, and like similar movements elsewhere in the Arab world, they became more frustrated with the older generation of Arab nationalists, who were seen to be a self-interested, self-aggrandizing, and corrupt barrier to true independence and economic justice. It would be this generation of Arab nationalists, who would begin to organize themselves into parties and organizations such as the Baath in Syria and the Free Officers Movement in Egypt in the 1930s, who would push aside the *ancien régimes* and their European masters after World War II. The final delegitimizing straw of the older generation, at least in the eyes of their younger counterparts, was their utter and abject failure in the first Arab–Israeli war in 1947–9, which led to the creation of the state of Israel in the heart of the Arab world.

Rebellion against and Solidification of French Rule

Traditional ethnic and religious leaders also opposed French rule, leading to a series of rebellions during the course of the mandate. The most notable rebellion began in the summer of 1925, when rebel Druze tribesmen drove the French out of the towns and villages in Jabal al-Druze. Curiously, the Druze were not necessarily motivated by Arab nationalism but rather by opposition to the intrusiveness of the French administration – which threatened the communal autonomy they had managed to maintain under the Ottomans – and worsening economic conditions.

This was a revolt of the underclass rather than one led by urban notables. The Druze were led by Sultan al-Atrash, who saw the benefit of working with non-Druze Syrians in order to aid the cause. The Arab nationalists in Damascus, seeing an opportunity to rid themselves of the French, called upon the Druze to liberate Damascus and initiated their own demonstrations in the capital. French military superiority, however, most notably on display with the bombardment of Damascus, squashed the revolt within a year. Although there were atrocities committed by both sides, the French employed particularly nasty tactics in putting down the rebellion, including assassinations, mass imprisonment and torture, and indiscriminate bombings of cities that killed many more innocent civilians than rebels. It certainly set an unfortunate precedent for future Syrian regimes attempting to stay in power. In the end, the revolt was brutally quashed with the French establishing a kind of police state in response, which hurt the local economy and led to the expulsion of a number of leading nationalists. It did, however, contribute to the development of a Syrian identity and, perhaps unintentionally, fanned nationalist sentiment, leading toward the formation of modern political parties.[5]

Although Franco-Syrian relations remained tense thereafter, especially when the deleterious effects of the worldwide Great Depression hit Syria in the 1930s, differences were generally played out in the political arena rather than on the battlefield. Urban notables formed a political party in the early 1930s that became known at the National Bloc (Kutla). It was primarily composed of landowners and merchants from the cities of Damascus, Aleppo, Homs, and Hama, and the overwhelming majority were Sunnis. This party would become the poster child of the older generation of nationalists, its members being perceived by many as more interested in maintaining, if not enhancing, their political and economic positions rather than attaining independence – or what was referred to as "honorable cooperation" with the French. And because of their origins and make-up, the National Bloc did not endear itself at all to minority populations in Syria such as the Alawites and Druze, nor did it attempt to really do so. This period was marked by slow progress in Syria's attempts to establish a political framework under which it could move toward full independence. A constituent assembly was elected in 1928, but efforts to draft a constitution foundered over the French high commissioner's refusal to accept several proposals and the assembly's refusal to compromise. One area of controversy was the Syrian insistence that all territories controlled by the French be considered part of Syria, thus denying the autonomy of Lebanon, Alexandretta, and Jabal Druze. In 1930, the French high commissioner dissolved the assembly and promulgated a constitution based on its draft, but without the offending articles.

The evolution of Franco-Syrian relations took another major step in 1936, when a Treaty of Alliance was established. The assumption of power in France by Léon Blum's liberal-socialist government also facilitated movement toward the agreement. The National Bloc agreed to cede the four districts that the French had appended to Mount Lebanon (Tripoli, Ba'lbek, Tyre, and Sidon) in return for the treaty, in essence agreeing to the formation of modern Lebanon. The Syrian parliament unanimously approved the treaty. The French parliament, however, never ratified it because the Blum government fell in 1937. With the prospect of war with Germany on the horizon, reducing the French footprint in its colonial empire was not on the diplomatic table for anyone in Paris, not just the colonial lobby. Despite this, it did serve as a basis from which future ties evolved. And with tensions rising in Europe, Paris ceded the province of Hatay (the Syrian province of Alexandretta) to Turkey in 1939, a move which further incensed the Syrians, and one that was only officially recognized in Syria in the early twenty-first century during an unusual – and what would turn out to be fleeting – period of warming Syrian–Turkish relations. The French essentially gave the province to the Turks so that they would remain neutral in the face of World War II. In addition to this, the National Bloc only gave lukewarm support to what is called the Arab Revolt in Palestine that broke out in 1936 and lasted for three years. It was quashed as efficiently by the British as the Druze-led revolt was in Syria in 1925 by the French. But increasingly the Palestinian cause became an important feature of Arab and Muslim grievances as well as a central element of several evolving ideologically based movements in the region. Fidelity to the Palestinian cause was *de rigueur* for Arab leaders. The National Bloc's relative lack of enthusiasm in the face of trying to get the treaty with the French passed and implemented did not go unnoticed.

Even with the continuation of sporadic French crackdowns, the fall of Paris to Nazi Germany in 1940 provided the opportunity for the Syrians to gain full independence. Some progress toward independence was made with the pro-Nazi Vichy government in Paris, which established partial self-government in Syria in 1941 after riots in Damascus. The Vichy appeared to be on the verge of allowing airbases of the Axis powers to be established in Syria. The British, heavily vested in the region, of course took notice. British forces along with the British-trained Arab Legion from Jordan moved into Syria to make sure it did not become a strategic threat. Promising independence in order to win popular support, they ushered in the Free French under the leadership of General Charles de Gaulle in the summer of 1941. Actual independence was in fact granted that September, but the French continued to act as a mandatory power. De Gaulle, ever the promoter of French empire, was reluctant to abandon Syria. Although an elected nationalist government came to power in 1943 under President Shukri al-Quwatli, with France according it most governmental authority, full independence was not achieved until after the war in 1946. Owing to British pressure and the reality of their weakened condition after the war, the French ordered their last soldiers to withdraw in April, and control of the *Troupes Speciales*, recruited mostly by the French from minority Syrian groups, was transferred over to the Syrian government.

Despite the often tense and antagonistic relationship between the French and most indigenous Syrians, the mandate period significantly influenced the country for decades. The Syrian educational system (particularly the private schools), judicial system, and many important sectors of the economy evolved from the French structure imposed during the mandate. Even culturally, French language, fashion, cuisine, and architecture are still seen in Syria today.

However, for the most part, French rule in Syria failed, certainly as strictly defined by the mandate system. There was very little preparation for statehood guided by the French. The lack of development of a class of skilled administrators in the ways of modern government would hamper Syria well into the future; indeed, political development was also impeded by the lack of a unified administrative structure in the country, due to the French "divide and rule tactics" for the better part of the mandate. The political elite therefore tended to act in a much more parochial manner than perhaps would have been the case in a more unified political and administrative system.

It would be difficult to overstate the challenges

facing this young, immature polity upon independence. It had just experienced the ravages of almost three decades of a rapacious and often ignorant supervisory power as well as the economic dislocation of a world war. There was no clear Syrian identity to speak of, and there were even some groups of Syrians who agitated for aligning – if not merging – with other Arab states, such as Iraq, Jordan, Saudi Arabia, and Egypt, who were themselves competing with each other. All of this amid an emerging Arab–Israeli conflict that would obsessively envelop Syria as well as a percolating superpower cold war that would soon impose itself with blind fury on a new country trying to find itself. It is little wonder that there was so much political volatility in Syria in the 1950s and 1960s. It would only end – for a time – with the coming of the military-security state, which seemed to be the sole form of government that could provide stability. It is to this story that we now turn.

4

Syria amid the Cold Wars

Syria emerged from World War II as a newly independent state freed from the shackles of the French
mandate. The country was now in the hands of a
group of politicians who had gained established positions of authority, if not some popularity, from their
long struggle against Ottoman and French control.
However, they had very little experience in the everyday operations of running a government and, in some
cases, had become disreputable in the view of many
Syrians for having cooperated with and been too conciliatory toward the French mandate regime in the
interest of obtaining and maintaining their political
and economic power positions. Being in charge of a
country with expectations to deliver services, economic growth, and national honor is quite different
than railing against the French as the opposition. But,
on the whole, this group, the National Bloc (Kutla),
was identified with the independence movement of
the interwar years, and as a result (also by default)
it maintained power immediately after World War II
under the guise of a parliamentary democracy led by
President Shukri al-Quwatli.

The 1947 parliamentary elections gave visible indications of the growing fragmentation of the Syrian

polity as well as the increasing public disappointment with the Kutla politicians. The election process catalyzed a split within the Kutla, leading to the
formation of the Nationalist Party (Hizb al-Watani),
which consisted of members of the ruling wing of the
Kutla such as Quwatli, Jamil Mardam, Faris al-Khuri,
Lutfi al-Haffar, and Sabri al-Asali, all of whom were
identified as Damascene politicians. The opposition
wing of the Kutla was based in Aleppo and counted
among its members Rushdi al-Kikhia, Nazim al-Qudsi,
and Mustafa Barmada. The latter group began to coa-
lesce in 1947 but officially formed a party, the People's
or Populist Party (Hizb al-Shaab), in August 1948.
Both parties were economically and politically conservative and tended to look to the West when military and/or economic assistance was sought, and in
the case of the Populist Party, its Aleppan base steered
it toward commercial relationships and an allegiance
toward the pro-West regime in Iraq (and toward frequently proposed union with it) that only distanced
it from the Nationalist Party over an issue that generally divided the Syrian political system, namely the
direction of Arab unity and the integrity of the Syrian
republic. This split within the Kutla and the antagonism between the two parties that emerged from it
would never be healed completely, and it would allow
the more nationalistic and leftist elements in Syria an
opportunity to subsume their own differences in their
ultimately successful challenge for political leadership.

The elections in 1947 also introduced most

Syrians to the Baath Party, an ardently nationalistic group operating under a pan-Arab socialist doctrine. It would systematically improve its power position in Syria to the point where by the mid-1950s it was virtually dictating the government's neutralist and largely anti-Western foreign policy. The Baath Party was essentially the product of the ideological meeting of the minds of two men, Michel Aflaq (a Christian Arab) and Salah al-Din Bitar (a Sunni Arab). At first flirting with communism while studying together in Paris at the Sorbonne in the early 1930s, both ultimately rejected communist doctrine and promoted the three interrelated ideas of Arab unity, socialism at home, and freedom from external occupation and imperialism. The Baath became the foremost proponent of Arab neutralism a decade before Egypt's President Gamal Abd al-Nasser made the term famous. The communists in Syria, small but well organized, were also opposed to the reactionaries and imperialists, but they were under suspicion from the Baath because their ideology was anything but home grown, and their actions were seen to be dictated by another outside power, the Soviet Union. They would, however, arrange a marriage of convenience at times when the country was confronted by the ominous and more imminent threats posed by the West and their "imperialist tools" in the Middle East (most particularly, Israel). They shared the objective of ridding the country of pernicious external interference and maintaining Syrian independence, but that was the extent of their cooperation, and when this objective was achieved their latent differences typically manifested themselves as an open breach.

The Baath might have remained an ideological party of the periphery if it were not for its association with the parliamentary deputy from Hama, Akram al-Hawrani, who ultimately provided the muscle for the organization with his close ties with various elements in the Syrian army, which would soon become the final political arbiter in the country. The relationship would prove to be symbiotic, for Hawrani's Arab Socialist Party was in need of an ideological foundation, one which the Baath was amply qualified to provide. Their formal merger occurred toward the end of 1952 while Hawrani, Bitar, and Aflaq were in exile in Lebanon, a propitious occurrence that had a lasting effect upon the future of Syria, for the new Arab Socialist Resurrection (Baath) Party (ASRP, or still simply referred to as the Baath Party) was now endowed with the political wherewithal to seriously contend for power in Syria, and it thereafter forced upon whoever was in power the increasingly popular foreign policy of strident anti-Zionism, Arab nationalism, and Arab neutralism. The Baath became the voice of the opposition to the West, Israel, and anyone in the government who was seen as collaborating with either one of them.

The seminal event during this period, however, was the 1947–9 Arab–Israeli war, which resulted in the emergence of the state of Israel in 1948. The regime of Shukri al-Quwatli was utterly discredited by its corrupt mishandling of a conflict that resulted in a humiliating defeat for Syria. (The repercussions were similar in the other Arab combatant states, Egypt, Jordan, and Lebanon.) The discontent among the populace and in the military and government created an opening for the entrance of the army into Syrian politics with the overthrow of Quwatli by General Husni al-Zaim in March 1949, a position from which it has yet to retreat. The coup signaled the end to Syria's brief encounter with parliamentary democracy and created the foundation for the important alliance between the Baath and the army in the 1950s.

The politicization of the army only exacerbated the divisions in the already unstable Syrian polity and added another player to the political power game. Indeed, the country's parochial and sectarian society offered ample fodder for the intrigues of foreign powers interested in promoting their own sets of objectives, and they could usually find willing partners in Syria eager to support these interests for the sake of political self-aggrandizement.

The United States was primarily interested in Syria in terms of the extent of the latter's growing relationship with the Soviet Union, fearing that it could become a Soviet client-state in the heartland of the Middle East, and, as such, a base for subversive activity. Moscow, in turn, did not want Damascus to become ensnared in any pro-West containment defense schemes developing at the time, and it wanted to extend its influence to a country that was more amenable to Soviet inroads than most in the region, especially as communists operated more openly there than elsewhere in the Arab world. France viewed its former mandated territory as its last area of ingress into the central zone of the Middle East and would, and did, do everything it could to preserve its largely fictitious position among the great powers in the area. To Britain, also on the wane as an imperial power following World War II, Syria at first was not that important, as London was reluctant to step on the toes of the French and was primarily concerned with its position in Iraq, Jordan, and Egypt. However, as its relationship with Egypt deteriorated, and as its influence in the region was being systematically diminished by the United States, Britain began to value Syria in terms of reducing Egypt's influence under Nasser, while at the same time enhancing its own stature in the area by augmenting that of its client-state Iraq, itself having a direct interest in Syrian affairs.

Turkey, already nervously exposed to the Soviet Union on its northern border, saw its southern neighbor as a possible strategic threat to its southern flank, especially with Turkish membership of NATO after 1952. Iraq was mainly interested in Syria in terms of its vision for Fertile Crescent unity and as a means to isolate Egypt in its drive for Arab leadership. Egypt, responding in kind in this regional cold war, wanted a country that looked to it rather than Iraq, as Syria held the key as to whether one or the other would lead the Arab world. Saudi Arabia was concerned about the disposition of Syria lest it fall into the camp of the rival Hashemite House ruling Iraq, enhancing that regime's stature and power at the expense of the House of Saud – thus for a time Egypt and Saudi Arabia cooperated in order to keep Syria and Iraq apart.

The generally pro-Western regimes of Jordan and Lebanon wanted a Syria that looked to the West but were not willing to take the initiative against their stronger neighbor and, for the most part, essentially hoped it would be a benign partner in inter-Arab affairs. And, finally, Israel wanted Syria to remain weak and non-threatening, hoping to create a more secure northern border zone out of the still unsettled border demarcation question that emerged from of the 1947–9 Arab–Israeli war. Like Turkey, the Israelis did their best to portray Syria as a budding Soviet outpost in the Middle East so as to tug at the hearts of an American public and government and gain valuable US political, economic, and maybe even military support.

As one can readily see, Syria was at the center of a tug-of-war with many different ropes and on several different planes. All of the international and regional interests that foreign parties held regarding the country were sometimes superimposed on, sometimes integrated into, its domestic political environment, simultaneously pushing together and pulling apart the fabric of its society in a complicated matrix.

The 1954 Parliamentary Elections

If the United States was worried about the leftist presence in Syria prior to the September 1954 parliamentary elections, afterward the situation was described as positively grave. Out of the 142 seats, the Baath Party gained an unprecedented twenty-two seats, increasing in strength from five percent in the previous parliament to fifteen percent in the new. At the same time, the Populist Party lost fifty percent of its parliamentary share, effectively ending political discussion in Syria on whether or not to merge with Iraq and forcing its supporters in and outside of the country to look to other, more covert methods to bring about union with its neighbor. And for the first time in the Arab world, a Communist Party member, Khalid Baqdash, became an elected official of government. In addition, Khalid al-Azm led a bloc of some thirty independents into parliament, and though the members of this group were seemingly conservative by background, they had cooperated with the leftists and campaigned on an anti-Western platform as well; indeed, Azm would soon emerge as one of the leading proponents in Syria of a closer relationship with the Soviet Union.

The disappointing showing by the conservative elements, particularly the Populists and the Nationalists, was due primarily to the antagonism between the two parties and widespread divisions within each, as well as the fact that they were identified with the West and, therefore, with Israel. The prevalence of rumors in Syria of American interference in the elections in support of pro-Western candidates did not help their cause either.

Since no one party won a majority in parliament, the stage was set for the formation of a coalition government. After several failed attempts by various party leaders, on November 3, 1954, the seventy-seven-year-old senior statesman Faris al-Khuri succeeded in forming a government consisting mainly of Populists and Nationalists. Although this seemed to be a reversal of fortunes for the leftists, it was really more the result of the fragmentation of Syrian politics, as the left-wing parties themselves were not immune to some of the divisions which had plagued conservatives; indeed, the leftist showing in the election spurred the Populists and Nationalists to bury the hatchet for the time being in order to form a government, although the veneer of cooperation wore off quickly. But the issues that the leftists had espoused were still more powerful than the tenuous make-up of parliament and the dynamics of Syrian domestic politics.

The Baath and Azm's newly formed Democratic Bloc refused to take part in the new government, yet despite the known pro-Western disposition of Khuri and the formation of a conservative-leaning coalition, the prime minister felt compelled to immediately and publicly proclaim his government's opposition to any "pledge, pact, or agreement" with a foreign power and its intention to improve relations with the Arab states and pay particular attention to the Palestine problem. The Baath's preoccupation with foreign policy, especially its anti-imperialist stance, and the pressure that it placed on Khuri was evident in the fact that it concentrated its efforts within the parliament to get its nominees elected to the foreign relations committee. The tide had essentially turned, and from here on out, with few exceptions, anti-imperialism and anti-Zionism became the calling cards for political success in Syria. As such, it brought Syria smack into the emerging superpower cold war between the United States and the Soviet Union and the regional Arab cold war between a rising Egypt under Nasser and Iraq under the pro-British monarchy. Domestic politics and foreign policy became inextricably linked together.

The Cold Wars in the Middle East Heat Up

The Baghdad Pact, formed in 1955, was a nodal point in the developing Arab cold war that would have serious repercussions for Syria. The Pact, later known as the Central Treaty Organization (CENTO), was a pro-Western defense alliance whose objective was to contain the expansion of Soviet and communist influence in the Middle East. It was part and parcel of the global containment strategy against communism led by the United States and its allies that also included the North Atlantic Treaty Organization (NATO), organized in 1949, and the Southeast Treaty Organization (SEATO), which came into being in

1952, forming a containment belt of sorts around the Soviet Union and the People's Republic of China. In a so-called "northern tier" strategy, the Eisenhower administration pushed for including non-Arab states, such as Turkey and Iran, in the Baghdad Pact so as not to become entangled in Arab–Israeli and inter-Arab tensions. The British, however, pushed to include Iraq in the Pact as a way to maintain their dwindling status in the region as well as potentially isolate Nasser by drawing other Arab states into the defense organization. To make a long story short, there were stronger voices in Washington advocating the inclusion of Iraq than there were for Egypt, the latter of which had been the focus of earlier attempts at organizing a pro-Western defense pact in the Middle East. So, contrary to the intent of the northern tier approach, an Arab state, Iraq, became a centerpiece of the Baghdad Pact, which was officially signed in March 1955.

Immediately, this upped the ante in the inter-Arab arena, which, in turn, intensified what Patrick Seale, in his landmark book of the same name, called "the struggle for Syria."[1] What London and Washington did not foresee with the formation of the Pact, which was focused primarily at the international level, was its regional repercussions, which actually led to the opposite of what it was intended to do. It was clear to Nasser what the game was now: he had to counter his deteriorating strategic situation by preventing his country's isolation. For Iraq, the game was to bring a few other Arab countries into the Pact. For Egypt, it was to prevent those very same countries from joining, and the key for both was Syria. It was the keystone in this Arab cold war. As such, there ensued a titanic – and mostly covert – domestic battle in Syria supported from the outside primarily by Cairo and Baghdad between pro-Egyptian and pro-Iraqi elements, with bribery, corruption, beamed-in radio propaganda, targeted violence, and political maneuvering charting the way.

Nasser was feeling the heat. Not only did he have the Baghdad Pact on his doorstep with his regional rival, Iraq, at the helm, but in February 1955 he had also endured an Israeli military action against Palestinian *fedayeen* (guerrilla) elements in the Gaza Strip, then under Egyptian control, who had been periodically carrying out raids in Israel since the end of the first Arab–Israeli war in 1949. Some forty Egyptian soldiers were killed, thus undermining Nasser's claim that he had demonstrably improved the military since the debacle of the 1947–9 conflict. In one fell swoop, however, Nasser turned the tide in his favor in this Arab cold war. In September 1955, he agreed to a massive arms deal with the Soviet Union, although it was officially through Czechoslovakia, a Soviet client-state. Nasser was a pan-Arab hero overnight. Finally, an Arab state was backed by a superpower and might have the wherewithal to undo the catastrophe, or *nakba*, of 1949 and take on Israel. For the Soviet Union, it was its first deal with a significant Arab state, leapfrogging the Baghdad Pact containment belt in the process, the exact opposite of what the Pact was supposed to do.

The arms deal, however, immediately connected rising tensions at the international, regional, and Arab–Israeli levels in the Middle East. The British, French, and, especially, the Israelis feared the arms deal had provided Nasser with the means to counter all of their interests. They had to strike before the Soviet arms could be integrated into the Egyptian military. In a nutshell, this is the origin of the 1956 Suez war. All the tinder needed was a match to light the fire, and it came in the form of Nasser's nationalization of the Suez Canal Company (owned and operated by British and French shareholders) in July 1956. This was a sufficient pretext for launching the tripartite invasion of Egypt at the end of October, a military operation born in secrecy, soaked in classic nineteenth-century European imperialism, and flawed by its very nature. With both US and Soviet cooperative pressure through the United Nations, a hard thing to bring about at the height of the cold war, the British, French, and Israelis were forced to withdraw after military gains in the first few days. As a result, Nasser had snatched political victory from the jaws of military defeat. If he was a pan-Arab hero following the arms deal with the Soviet Union, now he was practically apotheosized in the Arab world. He had taken on Israel and the traditional European imperialists and survived. He now had the upper hand in Syria against pro-Iraqi interests, and he succeeded in turning the tables on Iraq as no other Arab country joined the Baghdad Pact. The pro-British monarchy in Baghdad was living on borrowed time in the midst of the onslaught of Arab nationalism, or what many now simply referred to as Nasserism.

By 1957 the focus of political attention in Syria was in the foreign policy arena. With the pro-Nassser hysteria in the Arab world following the Suez war, the most popular political positions could not help but fall within this sphere. The leftists continued to promote anti-imperialist and anti-Zionist themes. They had, however, no cogent domestic political program and therefore relied heavily on doctrinaire enunciations having little applicability to reality. In addition, they still had to depend on individuals who by anyone's definition were rich feudal landowners (such as Khalid al-Azm) and thus reminders of the class of urban notables who had dominated politics in the major cities of Syria since the Ottoman days and against whom the younger generation of Baathists and other leftists had railed for years. It was no surprise then that they also focused on foreign policy issues as a practical matter.

The leftist elements in Syria used the post-Suez atmosphere to their advantage in order to consolidate power. They also benefited from and exploited the announcement on November 24, 1956, of the discovery of a British–Iraqi plot (Operation Straggle) to overthrow the regime. On December 11, the Syrian government, spearheaded by Baath leader Akram al-Hawrani and Khalid al-Azm, announced the formation of a parliamentary National Front pledged to follow an anti-Western, neutralist, and pan-Arab foreign policy opposing "plots against the State, imperialism, and the Baghdad Pact."[2] The great majority of the deputies in parliament supported the National Front, which signaled the formation of a strong left-wing coalition that would support the country's Baathist-inspired foreign policy and provide the unity necessary to withstand the danger posed by outside powers.

The result of this political maneuvering in Syria was that by the time the Eisenhower doctrine was announced in early 1957, which promised US assistance to any country in the region requesting it in order to fend off the advances of "International Communism," the Syrian government had already solidified its official neutralist line with implied hostility toward the United States. There could be only one response to the Eisenhower doctrine: rejection. As far as the Syrians were concerned, the doctrine was totally off-base because it focused on what Washington saw as the major threat to *its* interests in the Middle East – that is, the expansion of Soviet influence – and not on what the Arabs perceived to be *their* main problem – Israel and the pernicious influence and meddling of external powers. The only aggression the Arabs had experienced of late was that of Britain, France, and Israel attacking Egypt in the Suez war in addition to the British-sponsored covert efforts to undermine the regime – nothing emanating from communist or Soviet sources. Also, any regional interpretation of the doctrine concluded that it was anti-Nasser, and thus it was contrary to the popular wave of support in the Arab world for Egypt in the wake of Suez. To the Syrians, the doctrine was a unilateral action by the United States in its attempt to assume the imperialist mantle of Britain and France, and with the recent covert interventions by the United States in Iran (1953) and Guatemala (1954) fresh in the minds of Syrian leaders, the next assault might very well emanate from Washington.

It was symbolic of the lack of solidarity in the Syrian polity and cautiousness within the National Front, however, that the reaction by leading Syrian politicians to the Eisenhower doctrine was somewhat mixed. They did not know whether to reject it outright or leave the door open for possible compromise.[3] With the expressed aim of the doctrine targeting "International Communism," many Syrian officials of known leftist orientation went out of their way to proclaim to the world that their country was not communist and was in no danger of becoming so. One of the founders of the Baath Party, Michel Aflaq, stated that "communism is strange to Arabs just as the capitalist system is strange to them. They will not embrace communism just as they do not embrace capitalism."[4] They did not want the Eisenhower administration to make the faulty assumption that Syria had fallen within the Soviet orbit.

This hesitancy to take a stronger stand against the United States would dissipate later in 1957, climaxing with the American–Syrian crisis.[5] The crisis began officially on August 12, 1957, when the Syrian government announced the discovery of a US-engineered attempt to overthrow the regime, which the Eisenhower administration believed was close to becoming a Soviet client-state in the region. The next day the Syrian government expelled three US diplomats from Damascus; the United States responded in kind on August 14, declaring the Syrian ambassador and his second secretary personae non gratae. The Eisenhower administration denied the accusations and steadfastly held this incident out as a sign of unacceptable growth in Soviet influence in Syria, especially as the country's leadership was generally Baathist or pro-Baathist, the new army chief of staff, Afif al-Bizri, was thought in Washington to be a communist, and Syria and the Soviet Union had agreed to sign a wide-ranging economic accord a week before the crisis erupted.

With the Suez debacle so fresh in their minds, those in the Eisenhower administration were careful not to appear to be second-generation imperialists and therefore preferred an Arab-led response to deal with the situation in Syria through either diplomatic or military pressure. None would be forthcoming in the end. Nasser had long set the Arab nationalist tune, however, and no Arab state, not even pro-Western ones, was willing to cross the dominant pan-Arab trend in the region in support of US objectives against Syria. As such, the United States turned to non-Arab Turkey to apply pressure on Syria to rid itself of communist and Soviet influence. With the Soviet Union to its north, Turkey did not want to see a Soviet client-state emerge on its southern flank, so it was only too happy to move troops toward the border with Syria in an effort to intimidate the regime and embolden opposition elements. This was the trip-wire, however, elevating what was a bilateral and regional crisis into an international one. Soviet prestige was on the line, so Moscow came out with threatening noises against Turkey; in turn, Washington then countered in kind and started moving naval forces toward the eastern Mediterranean.

Below the superpower standoff, however, Egypt's Nasser was concerned lest he lose his influence in Syria to the Soviets, especially as Moscow seemed to be coming to the rescue of the Syrians. In a display of bold sang froid, Nasser sent Egyptian troops to Syria in late October, ostensibly to protect the country from the Turks, even though the low number of troops sent (five thousand) was woefully inadequate for the task. However, it was not a military move, but a political one. It was made to shore up Egypt's position in Syria as the country that matched words with deeds, thus preventing the latter from being totally swallowed up by Moscow at Cairo's expense. Importantly, it was also a sign of support for pro-Nasserist allies in Syria, particularly the Baathists, who did not want to see the Syrian communists improve their position in the country at their expense, especially ahead of upcoming parliamentary elections. Even the United States acquiesced, as the Eisenhower administration realized that the enhancement of Nasser's position in Syria was the lesser of two evils; indeed, Washington officials began to recognize at a practical level that the Arab nationalists were not always in bed with the communists and were, for different reasons, wary of the Soviet Union.[6] The end result of the American–Syrian crisis laid the foundation for Syria's merger with Egypt in February 1958, creating the United Arab Republic (UAR), which on the surface seemed to be a harbinger of things to come in the Arab world in the heyday of Nasserist pan-Arab unity.

It was not. In essence, the UAR failed because the two countries simply did not fit, economically or politically. Nasser and his Egyptian cohorts came to dominate the province of Syria in a way that was distasteful to a number of Syrian parties, not least of which was the Baath, which had originally pushed for the merger yet soon became marginalized by pro-Nasserist elements; indeed, it was officially disbanded for a time by Nasser, fearing a legitimate threat to his political position. In addition, the UAR seemed doomed when it appeared that no other significant Arab country would join, especially after the revolution in Iraq in July 1958 brought to power those who were thought to be pan-Arabists. The pull of Iraqi nationalism rather than pan-Arab integral unity ultimately prevailed in Iraq, and Baghdad declined the invitation to join the UAR. State nationalism had trumped Arab nationalism, a dynamic that complicated allegiances in Syria and Egypt. Finally, in September 1961, following yet another coup by parties representing the traditional elite in Damascus, Syria seceded from the UAR. Although anti-Egyptian sentiment ran high for a time, the new regime was not really representative of the trajectory of Syrian policy prior to the UAR, and as a result, it would soon resume the more outward anti-imperialist, anti-Zionist, and anti-landed aristocracy direction characteristic of the mid- to late 1950s. The political immaturity and weakness of the Syrian state continued to create vulnerabilities that were taken advantage of by regional and international powers associating themselves with various factions in the country. The result would be continued political instability at the top that hampered socio-economic development outside of the large landowning and commercial families, who effectively maintained a tenuous hold on power in Syria. These internal fissures allowed avenues of political upward mobility for new political groupings, however, who could, through targeted alliances with factions of the military, navigate the political labyrinth toward acquiring power themselves. One such group was the Baath Party.

5

The 1967 Arab–Israeli War

As detailed in the preceding chapter, there had been an Arab cold war since the mid-1950s. This is actually something Israel didn't mind at all: that is, as long as the Arab states were bickering amongst themselves, they would have less energy to focus on militarily confronting Israel. However, the more intense the Arab cold war became in the early 1960s at a number of different levels, the more opposition to Israel – in actions and not just words – became a litmus test of fidelity to the Arab nationalist cause, all the while heightening tensions at the Arab–Israeli level. Although they differed on means, hostility toward Israel was also about the only thing that the Arab states could agree upon, and the Soviets fed into this in order to align its allies in the Arab world more solidly behind the Kremlin in the ongoing superpower cold war. This was a dangerous game, though, as it built up expectations in Arab states that the Soviet Union would provide the necessary support for them to defeat Israel. Importantly, it also raised Israel's security concerns to the point where it might consider pre-emptive action to thwart what it viewed as an unfavourable balance of power.

The nature of the Arab cold war also changed in Syria in March 1963, when the Baath Party finally captured power in a coup. The very existence of Israel was anathema to the Baath. The party's Syrian founders, Michel Aflaq and Salah al-Din Bitar, were imbued with anti-imperialism as well as doctrinaire socialism. The Baath slogan of "freedom, unity, and socialism" betrayed the domestic as well as foreign policy applications of Baathist ideology. "Unity" in this sense meant Arab unity, a necessity to fight off the pernicious advances of European imperialism – and, in the post-World War II period, the cold war interference of the superpowers.

Israel was viewed as a wedge to Arab unification, the culmination of which would be an Arab nation united under one flag, leadership, and ideological structure; this would remake the Arab world into a global force. Western imperialism had, in the Baath perspective, planted Israel in the heartland of the Arab world, perhaps purposely, in order to keep the Arabs divided. One of the main prescriptions for curing the Arab world's weakness was, therefore, simply the elimination of Israel. In reality, however, although an easy target, Israel had little to do with a good portion of the continued Arab divisiveness in the 1950s and early 1960s.

The immediate aftermath of the March 1963 coup was the "volcanic" period of the Baathist revolution. Coming on the heels of a Baath coup in Iraq in the previous month, this series of events was seen by Baathists everywhere as a portent of things to come. It was a revolutionary period that withstood the setbacks of the failed unification talks with Nasser later in 1963, persistent intra-party divisions, and continued political immaturity. And as with any revolutionary period, at least in the eyes of those leading it, it was a time for aggressive implementation of policy on both the domestic and regional levels. Leading this charge was a dynamic Baath Party that is not the one that we see in Syria today, which has become a shell of its former self, a moribund state vessel through which power is articulated and from which power is co-opted.

The division and internal struggles of the Baath Party are the key to understanding Syria's role in the outbreak of the 1967 Arab–Israeli war. The political tumult in Syria fueled a growing Israeli concern that unpredictability in Damascus would generate an erratic, yet aggressive, foreign policy aimed at the Jewish state. Israeli journalist Zeev Schiff, who had close ties with the Israeli defense establishment, commented in 1966 that Syria was ruled by "unregulated Arab gangs. Even when there is a chance of reaching an arrangement along the border, we do not know if the person talking with us today will be there tomorrow to fulfil his promises. Syria is dragging Israel into war."[1]

The Baathists were relatively unknown commodities in Syria, and it seemed they had to either fight off Nasserist coup attempts, as happened in July 1963, or keep a wary eye on their supposed Arab nationalist compatriots, who, according to the Baathists, had too easily accommodated themselves to the forces of reaction. Others suspicious of the Baath and its anti-capitalist policies were the Sunni bourgeoisie and traditional landowning families in Syria, who had agitated for the breakup of the UAR in 1961. The early to mid-1960s was a conspiratorial period in Syria. It was a political climate that bred paranoia rather than calm and stability among the would-be and actual leadership groups. Pitted against the Nasserists and the "reactionaries" (such as the pro-Western monarchies of Saudi Arabia and Jordan), the Baath Party succeeded in surviving, but in doing so it also succeeded in isolating Syria from much of the rest of the Arab world.

Within the Baath Party there were splits between the Military Committee and the civilian leadership, between older and younger party members, between rural peasant and urban intellectual party members, and between minority groups based on tribal and regional ties. Some of these divisions manifested in the different policy priorities of the Baath Party Regional Command and the National Command, in theory the overarching ruling Baath organ, which included Iraq as well as party branches in other Arab countries.[2] The differences were in some cases ideologically based, but they were also often based on power, ambition, and personal jealousies.[3] Remarking on the directional shifts within the Baath Party itself, historian Malcolm Kerr wrote in 1971:

They had no interest in courting Cairo's favour, and indeed there was more than a trace among them of Chinese-like contempt for 'Abd al-Nasir's Soviet-style espousal of peaceful coexistence. Although Ba'thists, they had left behind them the misty *Volksgeist* nationalism of 'Aflaq and Bitar and indeed the whole preoccupation with Arab unity which had dominated Ba'thist ideology from the beginning, and had become Marxist social radicals committed to the class struggle.[4]

The culmination of this internal struggle was the intra-Baath coup of February 23, 1966, the ninth time in the past seventeen years that the Syrian government had been overthrown by force. It was the result of a winnowing process of radicalization within Baath Party politics that was intimately tied to the military through the Military Committee of the party's ruling apparatus. The rivalries were marked by a combination of holier-than-thou political mantras and actions on the domestic and foreign policy fronts. Syrian leaders built alliances with military factions based on sectarian, tribal, and regional ties in attempts to isolate other factions. There were thus frequent purges within the military establishment, especially in the officer corps, in the period preceding the outbreak of the 1967 war. As sectarianism was believed to be detrimental to the welfare of the state and of the Baath Party, it was intensely frowned upon and railed against, yet at the same time it was being utilized to outmaneuver rival groups.

What began as a mighty battle that pitted Arab progressive forces against reactionary forces became an internal struggle within the progressive camp in the Arab world between Baathists and Nasserists. Upon the party gaining power, a fight for supremacy developed between the younger, rural, and military Baathists and the older, urban, and civilian Baathists which in many ways was also one between the Regional and National Commands. In the minds of the younger generation, the leaders of the older generation had obviously lost their way, and their ideas had grown stale since the party's establishment in the 1950s. The old guard, they felt, had abdicated their role when they willingly disbanded the Baath Party under Nasserist pressure during the time of the UAR (1958–61). It was time to restore a Syrian face to Arab nationalism.

This basic intra-Baathist division devolved into a struggle between minority (Alawite, Druze) Baathists, who tended to occupy a disproportionately high number of officer posts, and Sunni Baathists. Sunni Arabs accounted for about sixty-five percent of the Syrian population as a whole, yet were proportionately under-represented in the officer corps. Sunnis resented the dominance of the minority groups in the ruling apparatus. Personal rivalries complicated the picture, such as those which developed between Salah Jadid and Hafiz al-Assad and among the Alawites themselves based on different family and geographical origins. Throughout the early life of the Baath Party in Syria, there was a kind of domestic cold war based on religious and economic ideas, policies, and practices between the new radical ideology of the Baath and the still powerful traditional interests in the country, particularly in cities such as Hama.

This type of multi-layered political struggle in an immature polity was not conducive toward moderate policies; quite the contrary, they tended to be sidelined in favor of activism and bravado. The type of regime this political culture produced in February 1966 was what one of the principal historians of the era, Patrick Seale, called "the most extreme Syria had ever known, rash abroad, radical at home, engulfing the country in war, and attempting to refashion society from top to bottom."[5] The February 1966 movement has often been called neo-Baath, reflecting perhaps less a difference in domestic and foreign policy orientation from its Baathist predecessor than an intensification and more doctrinaire application of those same policies. Some may focus more on *raison d'état* pragmatism rather than radical Arab nationalism as the driving force of Arab policy prior to the 1967 war, as it most surely was after the war. However, while this may be true of Egypt, it is less true of Syria, where policy continued to be shaped by a confluence of forces, from personal antagonisms and sectarian politics to Arab nationalist ideology. The latter was the ideal, which, in the minds of the neo-Baath ruling elite, had been betrayed by previous regimes, Baathist and non-Baathist alike. Similar policies continued, but under the neo-Baath they would now be applied correctly and appropriately. It was a difference in style and form, not content. This approach, of course, is what eventually got the neo-Baath in trouble at home and abroad.

The February movement inherited a multi-pronged struggle against Israel. It took on several forms. The first was over the ability to farm, if not control, the agricultural lands in the three demilitarized zones astride the border of Israel and Syria established in 1949 after the end of the first Arab–Israeli war. The second was Israel's diversion of the headwaters of the Jordan River in its National Water Carrier project, and the Arab League-sanctioned Syrian response of trying to carry out its own diversion efforts of the river's tributaries running through the Golan Heights. Finally, there was the issue of Syrian support of Palestinian *fedayeen* attacks against Israel, usually from the direction of Jordan rather than directly across the Israeli–Syrian border. All these issues in some ways caused and in some ways exacerbated tensions at the Arab–Israeli level and, importantly, also at the inter-Arab level.

The Palestinian issue, particularly *fedayeen* raids, by default became a sanctioned Arab response that Syria eagerly supported under successive Baathist governments. The Baath Party, stung by the experience of the UAR as well as the failed unity talks with Nasser following the Baathist advent to power in 1963, was only too willing to call out the Egyptian president for doing too little, too late against Israel. It was a battle between

Syria and Egypt over who was actually implementing true Arab nationalist ideology.

The demilitarized zones were relatively small territories along the 1949 armistice line in which neither side was permitted to introduce military units; they were supervised by the Mixed Armistice Committees through the United Nations Truce Supervision Organization. These three territories had been placed on the Jewish state side of the line in the 1947 UN partition plan, but Syria had taken them by force during the 1948 war. The Israeli–Syrian armistice agreement in 1949 arranged for Syrian troops to be withdrawn and for the zones to be demilitarized. Though small, the territories were a source of contention, and neither side was willing to give them up voluntarily. There had been sporadic clashes between Syrian and Israeli armed units as well as civilians (or on occasion Israeli military personnel dressed as civilians) ever since 1949, with punitive raids by Israel in 1955, 1960, and 1962. Although largely condemned for these raids by the international community, Israel portrayed them as self-defense against both Syrian attempts to redraw the cease-fire line and Palestinian attacks.

The Syrians tried to take control of the Palestinian cause, shifting away from Nasser's more cautious approach by helping the Palestinian guerrillas "burst out of the Arab box" in which Nasser hoped to contain them and "develop momentum to the excitement of the Arab public."[6] Syrian support for Palestinian attacks against Israel was important, especially since

Jordan and Lebanon were doing their best to prevent such incursions for fear of Israeli reprisals. Indeed, more Palestinian guerrillas were killed by Jordanian and Lebanese forces before 1967 than by the Israelis.[7]

Since Syrians consider Arab nationalism to be their birth-right, it was almost a sacred duty to support the Palestinian cause, especially at a time when the elimination of Israel and the return of the Palestinian homeland were still considered viable options. Syria was the country that matched words with deeds, not Egypt, and Cairo was consistently criticized for restraining Palestinian activism. The Palestinians, hoping to engulf the Arab world in war against Israel – for that was the only way they would get their land back – were only too eager to embrace Syrian support for the time being. For the Baathists, supporting Palestinian guerrilla activity was a no-brainer: it was ideologically predisposed to do so; it made Nasser look impotent; it earned Damascus plaudits in most Arab circles; it gave Syria the upper hand ideologically in terms of Arab nationalism; it had practical application in the form of potential results along the border with Israel; and, since most of these guerrilla attacks directly emanated from Arab territories other than Syria, there was an element of plausible deniability.

The problem with Syria's aggressive policy was the inability to carefully calibrate it – that is, to accurately assess the reaction of the Israelis. It led to the development of what in Israel was called the "Syrian syndrome." Brigadier-General Israel Lior, military secretary to Israeli Prime Minister Levi Eshkol (1963–9), described this as something that typically affected almost anyone who served on the northern border with Syria: "Serving on that border, opposite the Syrian enemy, inflames extraordinary hatred toward the Syrian army and people. We loved to hate them."[8] Israeli hostility toward Syria led to frequent calls for a more muscular and punitive military response, if not all-out war, against the country in the weeks, months, and years preceding the 1967 conflict.

The Coming of War

Syria was severely unprepared for war. Despite the bombastic and jingoistic rhetoric, the Baathist regime viewed its actions against Israel as low-level warfare that was not meant to lead to all-out conflict. The months and years prior to the 1967 Arab–Israeli war were filled with military purges associated with actual and attempted coups that decimated and further fractured the military and party, resulting in an inexperienced officer corps as well as a deep distrust between the rank and file and officers in the army. In addition, there were uprisings by discontented elements of the Syrian population, less than satisfactory military encounters with Israeli forces, and indications that Soviet support was only lukewarm. Behind all of this was a budding rivalry between the two strongmen of the regime, Salah Jadid and Hafiz al-Assad, which was beginning to manifest itself. One would be hard-pressed to find a military less prepared for war with a clearly superior foe.

The period between the February 23, 1966, coup and the June 1967 war were beset by the difficulties of a new regime struggling to establish its legitimacy and authority. Soon after the coup there were, as one might expect in Syria, counter-coup attempts by elements loyal to former President Amin al-Hafiz and the National Command. Naturally, there followed a series of purges and arrests, which were particularly devastating to the Syrian officer corps. Over the next fifteen months, the regime was constantly on the lookout for coup attempts, especially by opponents who took refuge in neighboring Lebanon, Iraq, and Jordan. A conspiratorial mentality breeds even more conspiracy, and soon there were coup attempts by disaffected elements within the Movement of February 23. Most notable was an abortive attempt in September 1966 by Colonel Salim Hatum, a Druze; although his troops had been instrumental in the February coup, he felt marginalized by the new Alawite-dominated regime. Indeed, an intra-Baath and intra-military polarization between Alawites and Druze came to the fore in the summer and autumn. The subsequent purges in the military and the Baath Party were extensive. Hatum was able to escape to Jordan, from where he continued his diatribes against the regime. In one September 14 interview to the Beirut newspaper *al-Nahar*, he commented: "The Alawi officers adhere to their tribes and not to their militarism. Their concern is the protection of Salah Jadid and Hafiz al-Assad. The latest arrests comprised hundreds of officers of all groups, with the exception of the Alawis."[9] The lack of "militarism," particularly in carrying the fight against Israel and on behalf of the Palestinians, was a constant charge aimed at the regime by the opposition even within what had been its own camp. In a way, the pressure the Syrian regime placed on Nasser was a reflection of similar pressure the regime felt from its own opposition. The regime could in no way seem less than what it said it was or do less than what it said it would do, or it would leave itself open to propaganda attacks.

As a result, the support for Palestinian guerrilla attacks against Israel, mostly through Jordan, intensified, as did skirmishes along the border between Israeli and Syrian forces. This particularly became the case after July 14, 1966, when Israeli aircraft bombed and destroyed Syrian engineering works trying to divert the Banias River, one of the Jordan's tributaries. Two months later Israeli aircraft shot down one or two Syrian MiG fighter aircraft (depending upon the source). There were those in the Syrian leadership who were Maoist in their orientation toward guerrilla warfare and others who believed that, with Syrian support, the Palestinians could do to the Israelis what the Algerian rebels had done to the French by 1962: in other words, wear down an occupying force by attrition until victory was achieved. Damascus had published *Sawt al-Asafa* (Voice of the Storm), the newspaper of Fatah, Palestine's nationalist movement, since May 1965. Furthermore, the regime helped organize Popular Defense Army brigades, made up primarily of both Syrian and Palestinian union workers, charged with defending the Syrian homeland against "subversive military activities and external attacks."[10] In return for Palestinian assistance with reinforcing regime stability domestically, it appears that the Syrian regime stepped up its assistance to Palestinian guerrilla operations against Israel. Again, the relative domestic weakness of the regime as well as regional isolation forced it along a road of adopting more radical foreign policies.

One of the important antecedents of the 1967 conflict was a serious clash between Syria and Israel that took place on April 7 that year, an event that in retrospect began the march toward war. Israelis within the leadership at the time have since admitted to baiting the Syrians on occasion by provocatively sending armed tractors manned by Israeli soldiers dressed as farmers into the demilitarized zones. This was one such instance, this time on the southern tip of the Sea of Galilee. The Syrians predictably fired on the tractor, prompting a heavy Israeli air response in order to teach Damascus a lesson for its continued support of Palestinian guerrilla raids. The exchanges in the morning of April 7 escalated, and Hafiz al-Assad, who was commander of the Syrian air force in addition to being minister of defense, sent Syrian MIGs against Israeli air forces in what turned out to be a large-scale air battle. Six MIGs were shot down, and Israeli jets humiliatingly buzzed Damascus in the process. It was quite the psychological blow, an asymmetrical Israeli response aimed at deterring Syrian activities, conditioning the behavior of the Baathist regime, and possibly encouraging more moderate elements to launch a coup by discrediting the regime. On the other hand, support for Damascus streamed in from all over the Arab world, as Syria was, once again, matching words with deeds. Consequently, Nasser received some criticism for not having responded in accordance with the Egyptian–Syrian defense pact signed in November 1966.

It is under these circumstances that the infamous Soviet warning arrived on May 13, informing Egypt that Israel was massing troops on the Syrian border primed to launch a full-scale invasion. Despite repeated examination, there is no generally accepted conclusion as to who initiated the warning or why, and whether it was genuine or disinformation. What is clear is that Moscow was trying to protect the Syrian regime and ward off a potentially catastrophic war. It also appears that the warning did not originate in Syria, although it certainly did not disagree with the way the Soviets informed the Egyptians. Damascus stood to benefit from the warning in terms of both actually deterring an Israeli onslaught and compelling Nasser to take the initiative. What is equally clear in retrospect is that the Soviets, Egyptians, and Syrians were not expecting a full-fledged war to erupt. The Soviets became concerned that war could lead to a confrontation with the United States if they felt compelled to engage, a loss of prestige if they did not, and the possible loss of an ally in Damascus. The Baath regime feared the loss of power in the event of military defeat. The Soviet warning was intended to prevent all of this, but it led to something quite the opposite. Indeed, a spate of memoirs by key Syrian figures written after the 1967 war almost universally blame Moscow for mishandling the situation. Even though Syria must have known Israel was not massing troops, it played along with the Soviet warning because of a genuine fear of an impending Israeli attack. The problem for Syria was that the regime lost control of the course of events to the Soviets and Egyptians.

As already noted, Syria was utterly unprepared to fight a war. The mismatch with Israel in terms of military readiness and materiel capability was compounded by the political and military purges since the February 1966 coup. In addition, there was trouble in Syria itself. Small craftsmen, artisans, and other elements of the labor force had been manifesting more vociferously their opposition to the economic policies of the Baath regime, with strikes and protests becoming more frequent into 1967.[11] These were supported and egged on by the Islamist party in Syria, the Muslim Brotherhood, who, of course, were diametrically opposed to the avowedly secular Baathist regime. The domestic tension burst out into the open following the publication of an article in early May in the army weekly that denigrated religion as anachronistic.

This was followed on May 5 by an incendiary attack against the "'atheist" regime by one of the leaders of the Islamist opposition, prompting mass protests against the government over the next few days in Damascus, Aleppo, and Hama. As expected, state security services arrested hundreds in reaction.[12] Naturally, the regime blamed agents of imperialism for fomenting the unrest, and in this atmosphere, Syrian officials – and maybe even the Soviets – just might have believed it was true, thinking it might be a prelude to invasion. Whatever the cause, it certainly made an actual war less rather than more attractive to the regime given all of the liabilities, obstacles, and distractions with which it was saddled.

Syria and the War

The focal point of the crisis shifted to Nasser after May 14.[13] On that day, ostensibly in reaction to the Soviet warning, Egypt demonstratively mobilized troops and moved them into what had been the demilitarized Sinai Peninsula. His actions were in part an attempt to control the crisis and take it out of the hands of the unpredictable Syrian regime. As Nasser's confidant Muhammad Hasanayn Heikal wrote, "The Egyptian view was that if the frightened Syrians made a wrong move, they could get us all into serious trouble."[14] Maybe now it would be Egypt matching words with deeds. The pressure that the Arab cold war had placed on Nasser had finally boxed him into a corner from which he would not emerge unscathed. While the Syrians and Soviets saw his mobilizing of troops into the Sinai and the subsequent removal of the United Nations Emergency Force from the area as desirable actions that would help deter Israel, both were probably caught off-guard by his announcement on May 22 that Egypt would close the Strait of Tiran to Israeli shipping. This action constituted a *casus belli* for Israel and was in many ways the point of no return for Nasser. The rest of the story is well known. After some more political and military moves by both Egypt and Israel, in addition to failed diplomatic attempts by the international community to ameliorate the crisis, Israel launched a devastating air attack against Egypt on June 5 that largely destroyed the Egyptian air force. In effect, the so-called "Six-Day War" was over in a matter of a few hours.

Despite the November 1966 mutual defense pact, there had been very little coordination or consultation between Cairo and Damascus as the crisis escalated. A command and control structure that was inadequate to begin with had become abysmal following the Israeli blitzkrieg. Both Syria and Jordan were in the dark as to the extent of the destruction of the Egyptian air force. In fact, Egyptian propaganda led Syrian leaders to believe that they needed to join the fight as the Arab side was winning. Such was the destruction of the Arab command and control system that the Israeli air force was able to successfully carry out its mission against Egypt and return in time to take out the much

smaller Jordanian and Syrian air forces before they
had a chance to mobilize. With the Arab air forces
effectively eliminated, the Arab ground forces were at
the mercy of the Israelis.

Except for some sporadic Syrian shelling of Israeli
settlements along the border, Syria stayed pretty much
out of the war for the first four days. This did not
go down well in the Arab world, not least because it
was Syria's aggressive posture vis-à-vis Israel that had
in large measure brought about the conflict. But the
Syrians were confused by what they slowly learned
was the scale of the destruction on the Egyptian front.
Indeed, they were astounded. They did not understand what was going on, nor did they have the military experience and capability, especially in the officer
corps, to react to the new situation. With no air
support, how could they move forward against Israel?
They reasoned that if they sat tight, they could emerge
from the conflict with little damage. With Nasser possibly irredeemably bloodied, the path toward Arab
leadership would be open. Despite repeated pleas,
they were in no hurry to come to Jordan's aid either.
They also figured that they were operating under a
Soviet deterrence umbrella, knowing the Israelis were
hesitant to move against Syria for fear of eliciting a
Soviet military response, especially as Damascus was
so close to the border. In any event, it was assumed
that the natural defenses of the daunting Golan
Heights would make the Israelis think twice.

On all counts the Syrians were almost correct. In

many ways it was these very same calculations and conclusions that led elements of the Israeli high command to decide, after some heated arguments, to engage Syrian forces in the Golan Heights in the last days of the conflict. Even though it could come at great cost in both military and diplomatic terms, Tel Aviv simply could not let Syria get away scot-free. Some Israeli leaders believed that it was worth the risk of upsetting Moscow in order to gain the Golan.[15] Levi Eshkol himself stated that "The Syrians cannot be allowed to parade in victory. . . . Israel cannot have overturned all the Arab countries and not Syria."[16] There were some ferocious battles on tough terrain in which the Syrians fought much more tenaciously than anyone could have anticipated and which were costly to the Israelis. Indeed, Israeli Defense Minister Moshe Dayan commented that "The Syrians are battling like lions." After buying time diplomatically in the United Nations with a cease-fire, and having been reinforced by troops and armor from the other fronts of the war which were now quiet, the Israelis were able to take the Golan Heights by June 10. The admirable performance by Syrian foot-soldiers in the Golan was erased by miscommunication and ineptitude in the officer corps and in the high command, ending ultimately in an uncoordinated and chaotic retreat from the region, including the city of Qunaytra. Once the prize of Qunaytra was taken, Israel – which was under severe pressure from the United States, the United Nations, and the Soviet Union – finally halted its advance. The

Soviets broke off diplomatic relations with Israel on
June 10 to register their displeasure with its actions in
the Golan and to make sure it went no further, especially as the road to Damascus lay wide open.

The Aftermath

In terms of personnel, materiel, and even territorial
losses, Syria fared much better than Jordan or Egypt
in the confrontation with Israel. Perhaps because it
could live with the postwar status quo, certainly more
so than Egypt with the loss of the Sinai, it could afford
to be less conciliatory in defeat than the other Arab
combatants. Syria had, however, indeed suffered a
strategic loss; after all, it had lost the high ground of
the Golan to Israel, as well as control of the tributaries that fed into the Jordan River, and now Israeli
forces were within earshot of Damascus. The intelligence capabilities of Israel vis-à-vis Syria were also
greatly enhanced, especially so after they occupied
Mt. Hermon on June 12, two days after the cease-fire.
Located at the apex of the Syrian–Lebanese border,
it gave Israel a clear visual and electronic view of
Syrian troop movements and communication traffic
in the south throughout the plains that surrounded
Damascus.

In Syria, as in other Arab countries, there were
desperate – and creative – attempts to mask the scale
of the overall defeat. In Egypt, the Nasserist regime
loudly asserted that the Americans and British actively

engaged in the war. In Syria, on the other hand, the Baathist regime proclaimed victory and tried to convince a skeptical Syrian public that even though it had lost the Golan Heights, the primary Israeli objective was to enter Damascus and overthrow the regime itself; since that did not happen, Syria was able to foil Israeli plans. Bemoaning this attempted regime spin, Mustafa Tlas, a member of the Baath Military Committee and an Assad confidant at the time of the conflict, wrote with "grief" in his memoirs that he would "never forget the words of [Syrian] Prime Minister Yusuf Zuayyin: Praise be to God, Qunaytra has fallen but the regime has not."[17] Needless to say, not many people in Syria accepted Zuayyin's optimistic portrayal of events. As such, a regime that had difficulty establishing its legitimacy prior to June 1967 was now fighting a rear-guard action just to try to stay in power.

As expected, recriminations flew back and forth within the regime itself, with the civilian leadership blaming the military leadership and vice versa. There were also a number of regime adversaries who had been let out of prison or exiles clamouring to come back into (and some actually entering) the country during the war to fight. They now saw an opportunity for a coup against a potentially disgraced regime; indeed, some were approached by dissatisfied elements *during* the war itself to overthrow the regime, but they wisely demurred for the time being. It was as clear an indication as any that to some notable Syrians, the primary battles to be fought were now inside the country's borders. In the end, the regime loyalists temporarily rallied around the flag of self-preservation; to do otherwise would mean their own demise.

In the internal power struggle, Hafiz al-Assad eventually triumphed over Salah Jadid in 1970. Assad viewed the domestic, regional, and international arenas much more pragmatically. He had seen first-hand how a reckless foreign policy could lead to unforeseen – and disastrous – results. Soon after the war he began to play the Syrian political game much more seriously, gathering up loyalists for an anticipated intra-Baath coup. It would take some time, and the Jadid regime maintained its radical positions in public forums, for instance rejecting UN Security Council Resolution 242 and pulling out of the 1967 Arab League summit meeting in Khartoum. There were moderate voices (Arab and Israeli) who believed in the immediate aftermath of the war that a peaceful resolution could be found. Syria was, for the most part, an exception. It is interesting to note that in a conversation with King Hussein, Syrian President Nur al-Din al-Atasi mentioned the possibility of a "moderate solution," but that he believed the Syrian government, as relayed by Hussein in a meeting with President Lyndon Johnson at the White House on June 28, 1967, "could already be too much prisoners of their own propaganda to make this possible."[18] The Jadid regime had become captive of its own rhetoric and policies – it still could not pull back from this.

For a variety of reasons, many of which had little to do with Israel, Syria played a very dangerous game. Its political-cultural landscape, characterized by intense political competition and at least the appearance of ideological fidelity among the political elite, won out over pragmatism and advanced radical policies at home and regionally. But the Syrians did not want war with Israel and thought they could get away with it. And judging from what appears to have been Israeli hesitancy, waffling, and extemporaneousness on the question of whether to take the war to Syria in the latter stages of the conflict, the Baathist regime, in fact, almost *did* get away with it. The Syrians assumed the Soviets, or at least the Egyptians, would protect them. As the crisis heated up in May, the Syrians let it be known to anyone listening that they had unlimited political and military support from the Soviets. They probably were trying to deter the Israelis, but they may have actually believed it. In addition, rather than seeing the November 1966 Egyptian–Syrian defense pact for what it really was – Soviet and Egyptian attempts to control the reckless behavior of Damascus – they tended to see it as a reinforcement of their strategic policy. Syria, after playing the cold war game to its apparent advantage, mistakenly presumed that its patron, the Soviet Union, would go much further than it was prepared to go to protect its client. Only five years after the Cuban missile crisis, while Moscow perhaps was not prepared to allow Syria to be destroyed, it was quite wary of the neo-Baath regime and was certainly not willing to risk World War III to save the Golan Heights. Mistaken assumptions were behind the anger of many Syrian officials at what the Soviets did and did not do in 1967, but it is equally clear that Syrian naïveté regarding regional and international politics led them to make these mistaken assumptions in the first place and to embark upon a reckless foreign policy bereft of military teeth.

However one chooses to see Israel in all of this, as a country reluctantly acting in self-defense against Arab aggression or as a hawkish, expansionist state taking advantage of, if not helping to create, an opportune moment, the Syrians provided grist for the mill. Syria was, by far, the weaker state when compared to Israel. Its actions against Israel made it that much easier for the hawkish voices in Israel to rise to the fore and implement policies that led to military triumph. The Syrians gambled, but the Israelis ultimately went all in and called their bluff. Syria paid for its misjudgment with the loss of the Golan.

6

Syria under Hafiz al-Assad

The name "Assad" (*Asad*) means "lion" in English; as such, Hafiz al-Assad, over his long tenure in power, became known in the Middle East as the "lion of Damascus." He was born in 1930 in Qurdaha, a typically poor Alawite village in the mountains marking off the coastal plain to the east of the port city of Latakia. For centuries this had been the Alawite hinterland. The first of his family to receive a formal education, Assad entered the military academy in 1952, graduating as a military pilot with the rank of lieutenant in 1955. As with many other Alawites, he used his military career as one of the few avenues of upward social mobility for minorities in Syria. He was thus in an advantageous position as he rose through the ranks when the military symbiotically converged with party politics in the 1950s, bringing people like Assad along for the ride. He had joined the fledgling Baath Party in 1946, and would become one of its rising stars, eventually emerging as one of the leading elements of the new Baathist regime when it came to power in March 1963. He was named commander of the Air Defense Forces as well as minister of defense by 1966, which provided him with a front-row seat for the 1967 Arab–Israeli war.

Hafiz al-Assad came to rule Syria via a 1970 intra-Baath coup that cast out the radical wing of the party, which had been ideologically committed to the destruction of Israel. The dangerous policies of the radical wing described in the previous chapter resulted in Syria's loss of the Golan Heights to Israel in the 1967 war. Assad's assumption of power signaled an effective departure from an ideologically based foreign policy to a more pragmatic one that was prepared to diplomatically resolve the Arab–Israeli conflict, albeit from a position of strength. Domestically, it also signaled a retreat from the radical socialist-based economic policies of the previous regime; indeed, Assad's political program upon his ascension to power is called the Corrective Movement (*al-harakat al-tashishiyya*). Its primary intent was to bring Syria back within accepted parameters in the Arab world and open up the economy to the private sector. Politically it meant establishing a working relationship with Egypt and Saudi Arabia (the so-called "Cairo–Damascus–Riyadh axis") in order to coordinate policy toward Israel.

This cooperative arrangement came to fruition in the 1973 Arab–Israeli war, when Saudi Arabia deployed the oil weapon toward the latter stages of the conflict, resulting in the almost four-fold increase in the price per barrel of oil. The non-oil-rich Arab states that bordered Israel, such as Syria and Egypt, benefited from the new economic realities in the Middle East, not only from direct aid from the large Arab oil-producing countries seeking to build up their Arab credentials the only way they could, but also from remittances from their citizens who were arriving by the tens of thousands in the Arab Gulf states as laborers. The 1970s thus resulted in impressive growth in the Syrian economy. In fact, Assad's decision to open up the economy to allow more flexibility for the private sector was less a reaction to the inability of the public sector to accumulate capital (as would be the case in the 1980s) than it was a means to find mechanisms to distribute the wealth suddenly entering the country; however, this growth was not structurally stimulated, but was due largely to Arab transfers and good seasonal rainfalls. It was a fortuitous turn of events that helped the Syrian president consolidate his rule. But it would not last.

Black September (or the Jordanian Civil War)

The highest proportion of Palestinian refugees following the 1947–9 Arab–Israeli war relocated to (or found themselves in) the Hashemite Kingdom of Jordan. It was somewhat natural then that the Palestine Liberation Organization (PLO), founded in 1964 to represent the interests of the Palestinian people, established its headquarters there. To most Jordanians, however, the PLO had become a state within a state, and it carried out guerrilla attacks against Israel that were inimical to Jordanian interests.

In August 1970 the United States brokered a

cease-fire to a low-level Egyptian–Israeli cross-border war known as the War of Attrition. For some Palestinians, it was an opportune moment to act. It was imperative to disrupt any momentum toward Arab–Israeli peace negotiations created by the cease-fire. Consequently, a radical faction of the PLO hijacked four passenger airliners between September 6 and 9, landing all of them at an airport only about twenty miles from King Hussein's palace. The hostages were released, but the planes were blown up on live television for the world to see. This was an affront to Hussein's authority that he could not let pass, so he moved against the PLO militarily, launching on September 16 the Jordanian civil war, or what the Palestinians refer to as Black September.

The Syrians became involved in the civil war. The radical Baathist regime of Salah Jadid was still in power, and it had apparently not lost its enthusiasm to bring about the fall of the reactionary regimes in the Arab world. This seemed to be a golden opportunity to get rid of the pro-Western Jordanian monarch, gain more control over the PLO, and enhance the regime's credentials for leadership now that Nasser had lost a considerable amount of his luster. Damascus sent armored tank columns into Jordan to assist the PLO. Getting wind of this, Washington ordered the Sixth Fleet to the eastern Mediterranean as a warning to the Syrians. The Soviets then issued their own warnings against the United States in order to protect their ally in Damascus. Washington's bluff was about to be called because the Syrians did not cease and desist. At this point, the Israelis became concerned about the fate of Hussein. Israel did not want to see him fall from power and a more radical regime along the lines of that which existed in Damascus take his place. As a result, it began to mobilize its military against Syria. Sitting in Damascus, the commander of the Syrian Air Defense Forces, Hafiz al-Assad, realized the seriousness of Israeli intentions. He disobeyed orders from Jadid to launch air strikes in Jordan because he believed – with some justification – that Israel would then intervene against Syria. In effect, it was the first salvo in what would become an intra-Baath coup d'état that Assad would initiate against Jadid soon after the civil war ended.

With Israel deterring the Syrians and Washington professing its support, King Hussein's forces defeated the PLO. Although the vast majority of Palestinian refugees would remain in Jordan, the PLO infrastructure was evicted by the middle of 1971 and moved to Lebanon. Gamal Abd al-Nasser energetically negotiated an end to the civil war by September 25, but it was done at risk to his failing health; he died three days later. Succeeding him was an original member of the Free Officers by the name of Anwar al-Sadat, who would counter initial low expectations to carve out his own unique legacy. In Syria, Assad pushed aside the Jadid regime in November, formally assuming the office of president in Damascus in March 1971.

The 1973 Arab–Israeli War and Its Aftermath

Sadat knew that the legitimacy of his regime rested on his ability to return the Sinai Peninsula to Egyptian control. The reacquisition of the Sinai was not only a political and psychological necessity, but would also bring economic benefits by reopening the Suez Canal and restoring control of the oil fields. The Egyptian president attempted diplomatic means to settle the issue, but Israel was not budging. So then he chose the war option to break the diplomatic stalemate. The result would be the 1973 Arab–Israeli war.

One of the biggest questions surrounding the success of the Arab combatants at the outset of the war is how Israel was caught so off-guard. This occurred primarily because Israeli officials were convinced that the Arabs would not initiate an all-out war unless they knew they could win. Every intelligence estimate concluded that no combination of Arab states could defeat Israel. Sadat, however, did not launch the war on October 6, 1973, to defeat Israel or even to regain the territory lost in 1967. He did it to achieve the more limited objectives of reactivating diplomacy by awakening the superpowers from their slumber and improving, if possible, Egypt's bargaining position with Israel. This is where the Israelis failed: they lacked the political imagination to even conceive that Sadat would go to war with only limited objectives in mind.

The Arab side was also more coordinated this time

around. Sadat made sure that Syria was involved and that it would attack at the same time in order to force Israel to fight on multiple fronts. This was not the same regime in Damascus that had been at loggerheads with Cairo throughout much of the preceding decade. Moreover, Assad always felt a personal responsibility to secure the return of the Golan since it was lost during his watch, so to speak.

Sadat would utilize the newly developed Cairo–Riyadh–Damascus axis to launch a simultaneous invasion of Israel. On October 6, Egypt attacked across the Suez Canal in the south and Syria moved through the Golan Heights in the north, all of which was backed up by a Saudi pledge, as the swing producer in OPEC, to utilize, if necessary, the oil weapon against supporters of Israel. The early successes experienced by both Egypt and Syria in the war were primarily the result of deception and targeted military strategy.

As expected, after initial setbacks, on October 8 an Israeli counteroffensive began on both fronts. It was successful in the north against Syria, but it stalled in the south against Egypt. The only problem for Hafiz al-Assad was that, according to him, Sadat never informed him that he entered the war with only limited objectives in mind. Assad held no illusions about completely defeating Israel, but at the very least he wanted to regain the Golan Heights, a military objective he thought Sadat shared with regard to the Sinai. Even the name Syria has given the war – the October War of Liberation (*Harb Tishreen al-Tahririyya*) – suggests the clear objective of Assad to "liberate" the Golan Heights. Syria and Egypt were thus fighting with two different strategic designs after the initial assault, which caught Assad by surprise and undermined his own efforts to engage in a successful offensive in the Golan. The Egyptian strategy enabled Israeli forces to concentrate to the north to stall the more immediate Syrian threat.

This prompted the Soviets to begin a massive air-lift of arms and ammunition to Syria by October 10. Despite this, over the next three days, the Israelis had pushed on to seize territory as far as the village of Sasa, only twenty miles from Damascus. By this time, Assad was fully aware of Sadat's more limited objectives, and he later even learned that the Egyptian president had entered into diplomatic contact with US Secretary of State Henry Kissinger from a very early stage in the conflict. To put it mildly, Assad was furious, and the tone of communication between Damascus and Cairo quickly deteriorated as he (and Moscow) demanded that Egypt do something to take the pressure off Syria.

Against his better judgment, Sadat finally relented and launched an offensive in the south on October 14. The timing could not have been worse, for Israel launched its own second counteroffensive on October 15, emboldened by the US airlift that commenced the day before. While the front in the north remained rela-tively static, with Israel perched to move on Damascus itself if necessary, the south turned into something close to a replay of 1967 in the Sinai. Israeli forces decisively turned back the Egyptian offensive and approached the Suez Canal south of the Egyptian bridgehead.

Syrian and Egyptian forces were now on the defensive. It is at this point, on October 19, that the Arab members of OPEC launched the oil embargo. In addition, Moscow began to see the gains its allies had made earlier in the conflict on the verge of disappearing. The Kremlin began to make threatening noises about directly intervening in the war. In typical superpower escalating fashion, Washington responded in kind by putting its nuclear forces on its highest alert since the Cuban missile crisis. It also placed heavy pressure on Israel to cease and desist before World War III broke out. The combination of all of these compelled the superpowers to negotiate a cease-fire via the United Nations, passing UN Security Council Resolution 338 on October 22. Although there were a few more tense days of conflict and diplomacy, the war finally ended on October 25. Syria and Egypt lost considerably more men and materiel; but Israel was bloodied, and the Arabs could claim at least a psychological victory.

This new reality led to Kissinger's negotiating strategy that has often been referred to as the "step-by-step" approach, meaning that progress on the Arab–Israeli front would have to come incrementally – a comprehensive Arab–Israeli accord was too complicated to even be considered at that point. The result was a disengagement agreement brokered by Kissinger between Egypt and Israel in January 1974. The agreement,

often called "Sinai I," arranged for the separation of
Israeli and Egyptian forces with a UN-monitored and
-patrolled buffer zone in between. Kissinger was also a
frequent visitor to Damascus in an attempt to arrange
a similar disengagement agreement between Syria and
Israel. In the first half of 1974 he traveled to and from
Damascus no fewer than twenty-eight times and met
with Hafiz al-Assad for approximately 130 hours of
face-to-face discussions.

Progress was slow. Hafiz al-Assad would become
famous for his deliberate, if not stubborn, negotiating
style, which was on public display for the first time
in this episode. Moreover, with the oil embargo lifted
in March 1974, which was one of the primary objectives of Kissinger's shuttle diplomacy, and an array of
forces in the Golan that was less combustible than that
which existed along the Suez, there was less urgency
to consummate a deal with Syria. Kissinger, however,
kept working at it and a disengagement agreement
was eventually reached in May. It was important at
this stage to get another Arab state to sign along the
dotted line in order to allow Egypt more flexibility to
move forward even further, for it was the true prize
from Washington's perspective. The Syrian–Israeli
disengagement agreement was just such a vehicle for
Kissinger – it was an end to another means, while
Assad considered it a first step toward the return of
the entire Golan Heights. The Syrian president was
wrong, and it would be a lesson he learned early in
his tenure in power. Per the agreement, the Israelis

withdrew from their position near Damascus into the Golan Heights to allow UN Disengagement Observer Forces (UNDOF) to establish their position as a buffer between Israeli and Syrian forces. This disengagement agreement held up remarkably well until the outbreak of the Syrian civil war in 2011, and it was one of the success stories in UN peace monitoring. Despite the agreement, however, Syria could not continue along the path that Egypt seemed to be mapping out for itself, a journey that would take Cairo to a second disengagement agreement with Israel (Sinai II) in September 1975 and, ultimately, to the 1979 Egyptian–Israeli peace treaty, by which the Sinai was returned to Egypt and relations were normalized.

Syria had long considered itself the standard-bearer of Arab nationalism and the Palestinian cause – it absolutely could not pursue negotiations unless everything was on the table, and it could not allow for any other Arab state, most of all Egypt, to enter into separate agreements with Israel that would weaken the bargaining power of the Arab side as a whole. To Syria, of course, it increasingly became apparent that isolating Egypt from the inter-Arab system was an offensive strategy masterminded in Tel Aviv and Washington. From Assad's point of view, it was important to acquire more leverage in the inter-Arab arena to either disrupt an Egyptian-led moderate Arab consensus from emerging or prepare for the worst in case Cairo successfully achieved its aims. Assad believed that time was on his side, especially considering the enhanced wealth and power of the Arab oil producers that would provide the wherewithal for modernization as well as military parity with Israel. Syria's involvement in the 1975–6 Lebanese civil war, which ended in the emplacement of over forty thousand Syrian troops in Lebanon, as well as its continuing tussles with Arafat's PLO, can be seen within this prism of potentially shifting regional alliances to confront Israeli opportunism and prevent Syria's isolation.

The Effects of the 1979 Egyptian–Israeli Peace Treaty

The events of 1979 could not help but dramatically alter Assad's conception of Syria's role in the Middle East. In the face of losing the leverage of Egypt, Assad frantically searched for allies to confront an empowered Israel that could now focus its attention on the north. The "Steadfastness Front," including Libya, Algeria, and the People's Democratic Republic of Yemen, diplomatically fortified Syria to a certain extent, but these countries were largely on the fringes of the Arab–Israeli conflict. Syria even briefly flirted with an entente with its Baathist rival, Iraq, in the midst of Egyptian–Israeli negotiations in order to contain Israel, but it would be an association that inevitably floundered over continuing differences between the two countries, ranging from persistent Baathist elite quarrels and personal animosity between Assad and Iraqi President Saddam Hussein to more practical matters such as water-sharing of the Euphrates River.

Whatever slim reed of hope that existed for an Iraqi–Syrian rapprochement was obliterated by the culmination of the Iranian revolution in February 1979 and subsequent Iraqi invasion of Iran in September 1980. With the arrival in Teheran of the Ayatollah Khomeini, who was an avowed implacable foe of Israel and the United States, Hafiz al-Assad saw a definite convergence of interests, taking steps even before the 1980 Iran–Iraq war to develop a relationship that remains intact to this day; indeed, from Assad's point of view, Iran provided some strategic depth now that the multi-front approach against Israel was defunct. When Saddam Hussein invaded Iran in 1980, it made it that much easier for Damascus to openly side with the Islamic Republic. Syria could only play a leading role in the Arab world as long as Egypt and Iraq were otherwise occupied and/or had somehow decided to abandon the Arab fold. Egypt had signed a peace treaty with Israel and was ostracized and isolated, and now Iraq, partially in an attempt to fill Egyptian shoes, leapt into an unexpectedly protracted war with Iran.

Because of its support of non-Arab Iran against Arab Iraq in the Iran–Iraq war, however, Syria's position in the Arab world actually became more isolated in the early 1980s. The Gulf Arab states, on whom Syria depended so much for financial and political support, were consumed with matters concerning the Gulf and less so the Arab–Israeli arena. Iraq, ensconced in war, toned down its rhetoric and began cooperating with the moderate Arab states so as to buffer its ability to withstand Iran. This emerging moderate bloc in the Arab world also allowed Egypt to rehabilitate itself and quietly re-enter the Arab fold. By the end of 1980, Syria seemed as isolated as it had ever been. Clearly, Assad's diplomacy had failed. Egypt signed a separate peace treaty with Israel and yet no serious coalition of Arab states would align their positions with Damascus. Worse still, the attention of most of the Arab states, indeed most of the world, was absorbed by events in the Persian Gulf and toward South-Central Asia following the December 1979 Soviet invasion of Afghanistan – not the Arab–Israeli arena.

A tactical change was necessary from Syria's point of view. Israel's de facto annexation of the Golan Heights in 1981 reinforced Syria's assessment of its own weakened position in the region. Something had to be done, and it seemed to Assad that Syria would have to essentially go it alone in the region for the time being. He began to put forward the possibility of attaining strategic parity with Israel, not so much to defeat the Jewish state as to act as an effective deterrent while at the same time strengthening Syria's bargaining leverage in any peace process that might develop. To do this, however, Syria needed massive amounts of military aid from the outside. As a result, the Soviet Union and Syria began to build upon what had been a tenuous relationship, exemplified by the

1980 Treaty of Friendship and Cooperation signed between the two countries.

Syria's relative isolation in the Middle East was not its only problem in the 1980s. Economically, the decade was as bad for the country as the 1970s had been good. Not only were the structural defects and inefficiencies of Syria's state-dominated economy becoming obvious, but the regional and international political and economic environments exacerbated already existing problems. Most damaging was the precipitous drop in oil prices by the mid-1980s due to the world oil glut. Not only did this adversely affect Syria's own not-insignificant oil revenues, but it also reduced remittances from abroad as well as financial aid from the oil-rich Arab states in the Persian Gulf, who were already displeased with the decision by Damascus to support Iran against Iraq. Concurrent with this development was an unfortunate decade-long drought that devastated the agricultural sector. This had already been suffering under the regime's policy of import-substitution industrialization, which favored industrial over agricultural enterprises. In addition, the general Third World debt of the early 1980s reduced capital inflow, and the recession in the industrialized countries had negative runoff effects upon developing nations seeking outside investment. Finally, the winding down and end of the superpower cold war and subsequent retrenchment of the Soviet bloc deprived Syria of the military and economic aid it had been receiving in such large amounts earlier in the decade.

As a result, by the early 1980s Syria developed a severe balance of payments and foreign exchange crisis. It had become clear that the state could no longer be the engine of capital accumulation; therefore, the regime decided that the private sector had to be given more leeway to fill the capital void and the country as a whole had to create a more investor-friendly business environment to attract foreign investment. This second period of "opening" (*infitah*) after the Corrective Movement was brought about by economic crisis and not economic largesse. A series of decrees throughout the 1980s attempted to ameliorate the situation, launching Syria on the road of what has been called selective liberalization – "selective" because if Assad liberalized the economy too much or too quickly it may have undercut the public sector patronage system that maintained the regime in power. The subsequent "zigzag" approach to economic reform experienced some success, but on the whole, by the end of the decade, produced disappointing results.[1]

Also confronting the Assad regime in the early 1980s was a very serious internal threat from the Muslim Brotherhood (MB) in Syria, mirroring similar rising Islamist movements in other Middle Eastern states by the late 1970s. There were three main causes for the rise of the Sunni MB: the avowedly secular nature of the Baathist regime, especially one led by a minority schismatic Shiite sect, the Alawites, whom most Muslims do not even consider to be true Muslims;

the economic difficulties and disparities becoming more apparent by 1980; and the inspirational example of the Iranian revolution, which, although Shiite, still set an example of an Islamist movement successful in overthrowing what it considered to be a non-Islamic regime. No doubt the MB in Syria were also galvanized by the assassination of Anwar al-Sadat by Islamic Jihad elements in October 1981, which, of course, only made Assad more wary of his own predicament. After enduring a number of attacks by Islamic militants against various representations of the regime, Assad ordered a full-scale attack against the center of MB activity in Syria. The result was the virtual sacking of the city of Hama in February 1982, with anywhere from ten thousand to thirty thousand deaths – Islamist opposition virtually ceased to exist after this crushing blow, but Syria's reputation regionally and internationally suffered.

It was under these conditions that Syria encountered the next challenge to its position in the Middle East: the Israeli invasion of Lebanon in June 1982. Assad was determined to make the best out of a potentially catastrophic situation, but he would have to dig down deep into the resources available to him in order to weather another challenge to his position in the region.

From the Syrian perspective, the Israeli invasion of Lebanon was the expected repercussion of the Egyptian–Israeli peace treaty. It was thought that Israel, freed up on its southern flank, could now concentrate on securing its position to the north. To Assad, the invasion was an attempt to outflank Syria, something Damascus had been wary of for years, and a concern that, of course, precipitated its involvement in the 1975–6 Lebanese civil war. Syria seemed to be quite vulnerable with its regional isolation and domestic problems – to Assad, the timing of the invasion, coming just on the heels of the return of the final portion of the Sinai Peninsula to Egypt, was anything but a surprise. One could almost sense that this was something of a last stand for Assad, and he would fight tooth and nail to prevent an Israeli victory in Lebanon.

As is well known, what at first seemed like a repetition of the 1978 Israeli sweep of Palestinian positions in south Lebanon escalated into the elimination of the PLO as a force in the country and the placing in power of a Maronite president (Bashir Gemayel) who would be willing to sign a peace treaty with Israel. Assad's troops were compelled to fight the Israelis alongside the PLO, and they suffered severe losses on the battlefield and in the air despite determined resistance. As the full scope of the Israeli plan unfolded and as casualties mounted in and outside of Beirut, the international community, led by the United States, attempted to bring the bloodletting to a close, just as the Israeli forces stopped on the outskirts of the capital, hesitant to embark on a house-to-house expulsion of PLO and Syrian forces. With the United Nations hamstrung by an expected Soviet veto, the United

States, Britain, and France led a Multinational Force (MNF) into Beirut in August 1982 with the defined objective to escort the PLO forces out, which was accomplished in short order, followed by the departure of the MNF.

Whether Syria was directly behind the next important episode – Bashir Gemayel's assassination in September – is ultimately left to conjecture, for there were many factions in Lebanon that did not want an Israeli–Maronite triumph regardless of the position of Damascus, but it definitely benefited from the ensuing course of events. Shortly thereafter, in an act of revenge, Christian Phalangist units, apparently with a green light from Israeli forces, attacked two defenseless Palestinian camps in south Beirut, Sabra and Shatila, massacring hundreds, mostly old men, women, and children. The MNF, still anchored off-shore, felt an obligation to return to Beirut with the ill-defined task of restoring order to the chaotic situation.

The longer the US-led MNF stayed in Lebanon, the more it began to be seen, certainly from Syria's perspective, as a pro-Maronite, Israeli prop. The attempt by the Reagan administration to consummate an Israeli–Lebanese peace agreement negotiated in May 1983, without Syrian or Soviet participation, seemed to be a case of the United States trying to do diplomatically what the Israelis could not do militarily. From the point of view of Damascus, this particular approach also seemed to be a flanking operation against Syria through diplomatic means. Syria was left out, and if the supposed US–Israeli plan succeeded, its isolation would be complete, and its bargaining strength vis-à-vis a return of the Golan Heights would be virtually non-existent.

From this desperate position, Syria lashed out any way it could. Fortunately for Damascus, the MNF presence and extended Israeli stay in Lebanon were vehemently opposed by a variety of factions, such as the Druze, the Shiite Amal, and the emerging Iranian-backed Shiite force, Hizbullah, thus producing a coincidence of interests that Syria would employ to its advantage. It is in this atmosphere that one can read the April 1983 bombing of the US embassy and the October 1983 bombing of the US marine barracks in Beirut – and countless smaller attacks against what was perceived as a hostile and tendentious MNF – leading to the withdrawal of the MNF by early 1984. The factionalization of Lebanon due to the breakdown of the state and the subsequent external interference by a multitude of powers made a chaotic situation worse, and the opposition to the Israeli occupation increased, forcing Israel in early 1985 to withdraw further southward to the security zone it would maintain along the Israeli–Lebanese border until May 2000.

Assad had won. Through his strategic use of various Lebanese factions and the commitment born by being pressed against the wall, Syria emerged as the dominant power in Lebanon – its western flank was secure. And Syria's Arab credentials were somewhat restored for taking on Israel and the United States and not just surviving but emerging as the victor.

While Assad won Lebanon, the United States and Israel, relatively speaking, would win the PLO. In 1983 Syria fomented an uprising in Lebanon against Arafat's Fatah faction, in the process of which it brought together traditional radical factions of the PLO to establish the Damascus-controlled Palestine National Salvation Front. In the end, however, Arafat's popularity, or maybe it would be more appropriate to say his institutionalization, within the PLO as a whole prevented Assad's own outflanking attempt from succeeding. Syria's intervention against Arafat lost many of the points in the Arab world it had gained in Lebanon – the self-professed standard-bearer of the Arab cause does not foment intra-Palestinian discord that weakens the movement as a whole. By the end of the decade, Arafat had clearly chosen a negotiated solution to the Palestinian problem and situated himself within the moderate Arab camp. The Palestinian *intifadah* (uprising) begun in December 1987 further led to Arafat's revival as a negotiating partner, resulting in late 1988 with the PLO's recognition of Israel, acceptance of UN Security Council Resolution 242, and the renunciation of terrorism. Much to Syria's chagrin, the PLO became yet another Arab entity striking out on its own toward potential peace with Israel.

By the end of the 1980s, then, Syria's position did not seem to be measurably better than when it began. Iraq had emerged victorious in the Iran–Iraq war after

Teheran reluctantly accepted a UN-brokered cease-fire in August 1988 – and it was an Iraq that wanted to re-exert its influence in the Middle East. The pillar of Soviet support that had braced the teetering policies of Assad for most of the decade virtually crumbled with the coming to power of Mikhail Gorbachev in 1985 and the Red Army exit from Afghanistan in 1989, both of which led to a dramatic reassessment of Soviet foreign policy that emphasized a drawing down of Soviet commitments abroad, more concentration on domestic restructuring, and improving ties with the United States. This did not bode well for Syria, as Moscow first urged and then backed the PLO's decision to pursue a negotiated solution, and the Soviet Union also improved its relations with Israel. Gorbachev made it clear to Assad upon the latter's visit to Moscow in April 1987 that Syria's reliance on military force in the Arab–Israeli conflict had completely lost its credibility, and he went on to suggest that Damascus abandon its doctrine of strategic parity and seek to establish a "balance of interests" toward a political settlement.

In addition to these problems in the foreign policy arena, Syria's economy continued to deteriorate by the end of the decade, due in large measure to the concentration of economic resources toward the military in the attempt to achieve strategic parity with Israel. Compounding the continuing burden of an overly-dominant public sector were a number of problems inhibiting economic growth, including the following: the lack of a private banking system or stock market to organize capital; an inadequate regulatory regime and insufficient transparency; a private sector that was too fragmented to lead the way toward capital accumulation; rampant corruption creating prescribed entrances into the Syrian economy in connivance with government officialdom; and, finally, and perhaps most damaging of all, a population growth rate of about 3.6 percent per annum, placing more pressure on a dilapidated economy to keep pace.

Assad's Pivot

Because of his position at the end of the 1980s, Assad was forced to change his policy as dramatically as he had at the beginning of the decade – he took Mr. Gorbachev's advice. In 1989 Damascus re-established full diplomatic relations with Cairo. With an eye toward isolating Iraq and building bridges to the United States, Syria also began to improve its relations with Saudi Arabia. While maintaining the link with Iran, important because of its relationship with Shiite groups in Lebanon and remaining a credible military threat to Israel, Syria made a strategic choice to join the Arab–Israeli peace process.

To the rest of the world, the outward manifestation of this policy shift was Syria's participation in the US-led coalition to expel Iraq from Kuwait in the 1990–1 Gulf crisis and war. Not only was it participating in an alliance whose objective was to weaken, if not destroy, the war-making capacity of its arch-nemesis in the Arab arena, but it clearly situated Syria in the moderate camp in the Arab world and opened up the economic doors of investment and aid from the West and grateful Arab Gulf states. To the United States, although Syria's attachment to the coalition was mostly symbolic, it was the most important of all the Arab states. Since Syria had been at the vanguard of the "Steadfastness Front" arrayed against Israel, its joining up made the coalition seem as if it consisted of the entire Arab world against Saddam Hussein rather than the usual pro-Western suspects.[2] For Assad, establishing a stronger link with Washington was very important; indeed, some Israelis have accused Assad of engaging in the peace process not so much to redefine Syria's relationship with Israel as to improve Syria's ties with the United States and the West. Not only would this have economic benefits at a time when Syria desperately needed them, but it was thought likely that Washington, keen to maintain Assad's engagement in the peace process, would act to curtail Israeli pressure.

In the wake of the Gulf war, Syria emerged as the key Arab player in the convening of the Madrid peace conference in October 1991, co-sponsored by the United States and the Soviet Union and including a Lebanese delegation (clearly acting under the direction of Damascus) and a Jordanian delegation that also consisted of Palestinian representatives from the occupied territories. For the first time, Syrian officials publicly sat down with Israeli officials to discuss peace. Even though the exchanges between the participants were more acrimonious than civil, a truly comprehensive peace process was underway, and the Arab parties continued to meet separately with Israel in Washington, paralleled by multilateral talks at various locales focusing upon such issues as arms control, trade, and water-sharing.

The Israeli–Syrian track would soon be overshadowed by the September 1993 Israeli–PLO Declaration of Principles, largely negotiated outside of the Madrid framework, and then the 1994 Jordanian–Israeli peace treaty. Assad was furious with both Arafat and King Hussein for, in his view, doing something very similar to what Sadat had done. On the other hand, now that the PLO and Jordan had signed accords with Israel, no longer would Damascus feel completely obligated to subscribe to the Palestinian or Arab nationalist line, for the PLO itself had compromised its position. Though bereft of some of its bargaining power, Syria now felt free to pursue its own interests.

Amidst constant delays in implementing the Israeli–PLO Declaration of Principles, progress on the Israeli–Syrian track was made, particularly on security issues.[3] After the assassination of Israeli Prime Minister Yitzhak Rabin in November 1995 by an Israeli right-wing settler, the Israeli–Syrian track accelerated under his successor, Shimon Peres. The rapidity of the push by Peres was at odds with the incremental negotiating tactics that Assad preferred.

But any prospects for the conclusion of an agreement in the short term were derailed by the election of Likud Party leader Benjamin Netanyahu as Israeli prime minister in May 1996. He immediately took a more hardline stance vis-à-vis Syria, stating what became the mantra of his tenure in power, namely "peace with security," and no withdrawal from the Golan Heights. For the remainder of Netanyahu's tenure in power, both tracks stalled.

The Syrian–Israeli track received a boost when Rabin's protégé in the Labor Party, Ehud Barak, convincingly won the election for prime minister in May 1999. He ran on a platform of carrying the peace process forward, and like Rabin, he also preferred the relatively less complicated Syrian track over the Palestinian one. With the Clinton administration acting as facilitator, the two sides engaged in serious negotiations, highlighted by Barak's meeting with Syrian Foreign Minister Farouk al-Sharaa in West Virginia in December 1999. The noticeable decline in Assad's health amidst his desire to secure an agreement before his untested son, Bashar, might have to take over the reins of power was an added inducement. Again, however, by early 2000, the negotiations had unraveled. An ill-timed leak in Israel of a draft agreement between Syria and Israel, outlining some significant concessions by Damascus and probably designed to drum up domestic support for Barak, embarrassed Assad. It compelled him to lurch backward away from the negotiating table. An attempt by President Clinton to heal the rift by meeting with Assad in Geneva in March 2000 failed. Assad's death in June from natural causes obviously ended the prospects for an accord.

Again, it seemed, the policy track adopted by Syria at the beginning of the decade had paid less-than-expected dividends by its end. For Syrians this was particularly galling. They felt that they were the key to convening the Madrid process, and what did they have to show for it? The PLO had an accord with the Israelis, Jordan had a peace agreement with Israel, and Lebanon had finally seen the Israel Defense Forces' withdrawal from the south, the latter removing one of Syria's primary bargaining chips vis-à-vis Israel regarding withdrawal from the Golan Heights. On top of this, the economy was in virtual shambles. The May 1991 investment law #10 was supposed to establish the standard for Syria's opening up to foreign investment. At the time, this was hailed as an important step in the economic liberalization of the country, but only if it were followed up with other necessary economic reforms, such as a legitimate regulatory regime, greater transparency, and real privatization. But for the remainder of Assad's time in power, nothing much happened in terms of economic liberalization. The brief economic upturn in the early 1990s was due not so much to an intrinsically strong economy as to the economic windfall of financing and investment from the European Union and the Arab Gulf states, especially for infrastructural projects, as compensation for Syria's participation in the Gulf war coalition. Economic growth dropped precipitously thereafter.

The Nature of the State

Syria under Hafiz al-Assad has been variously described as a family-run business (akin to the Mafia), a crony-ocracy, and/or a *mukhabarat* or security state. None of these are particularly positive references; indeed, they refer to what is popularly perceived to be a repressive and corrupt state apparatus that first and foremost is built for and tailored toward the primary objective of staying in power. A more academic description would say that Syria under Assad developed into a neopa-triarchal state. This essentially means that he became a father-ruler, what Hisham Sharabi would call "a modernized version of the traditional patriarchal sul-tanate" that existed for centuries in the Middle East.[4] In other words, Assad adopted the position of the "sultan" under the guise of a modern political system, in this case a parliamentary republic with a consti-tution full of caveats. A carefully constructed system of patron–client relationships tied various important sectors of society into the ruling system, co-opting them into supporting the father-ruler and his cronies, who were often family members.

To keep the system in working order, and the populace as a whole obedient, the *mukhabarat* was empowered to carry out the dictates of the regime and protect it against real and imagined threats. As Sharabi goes on to state, "A two-state system prevails in all neopatriarchal regimes, a military-bureaucratic structure alongside a secret police structure, and the latter dominates everyday life."[5] While without doubt Syria is located in a dangerous neighborhood and has been involved in numerous Middle Eastern conflicts, critics of the Assads have asserted that the perceived threat to the regime is consistently exaggerated in order to consecrate the necessity for the security state. The typical refrain from government mouthpieces is that it is needed to protect the state from external threat as well as provide order and stability to a multi-ethnic and multi-religious entity whose natural condition without it would be chaos and violence.

Hafiz al-Assad liked to think he ruled through institutions, many of which he inherited from the Baath Party system that had been in place. As Patrick Seale wrote: "He [Assad] wants people to believe in his institutions: the popular organizations, the people's assembly [parliament], the National Progressive Front [government-sanctioned coalition of political parties], the local government bodies and, above all, the legitimacy of his own election to the presidency."[6] It is through these institutions that he believed the people participated in government, but his understanding of democracy was incomplete at best, and it had been shaped in part by the ruthless and conspiratorial politics of Syria since independence. So while there were, indeed, elements of participatory government, especially at the municipal level, it was sanctioned and controlled in a way that ensured the continuance of the Baath Party in power as well as the Assad family. And there developed a self-serving paternalistic attitude toward most of the Syrian population that it was, on the whole, incapable of prudent governance; therefore, in a classic patriarchal manner, it had to be led – and disciplined – when necessary in order for the country to function. For the most part, the people bought into or had no choice but to accept this Faustian bargain: that is, in return for stability and the opportunity for a decent living, they would give up certain freedoms.

The elections themselves betrayed the nature of the beast. The Syrian presidential elections under Assad occurred every seven years. They were, in fact, referendums rather than elections. Typically, there were no other candidates, and the ballot consisted of ticking off a "yes" or a "no" in an open voting environment. It would indeed be the intrepid voter, no doubt with security looking on, who would vote "no." This system usually garnered between a ninety-seven and a ninety-nine percent vote for "election" to another seven-year term.

In essence, the Baath Party became a party of government. In fact, it became something of a shadow government that operated in parallel to the regular government. The Syrian government had a Cabinet with a prime minister and a variety of other ministries, each with their separate buildings housing them, but at Baath Party headquarters in Damascus there were party heavyweights who held portfolios that were the same as or similar to those of the various Cabinet ministers. They are the ones who really wielded the power. There was also a clique of military and security generals, most of whom were unknown to outsiders, who answered directly to the president and when necessary trumped all except the president on important matters of state. While many of the government ministers were not Alawites, most of the security chiefs and generals were; more specifically, they were generally Alawites who were connected to Assad via clan relations and/or geographic proximity in terms of place of origin. Finally, the regime navigated and negotiated alliances with tribes in Syria, especially those located in the eastern portions of the country toward the Iraqi border. Through persuasion, bribery, diplomacy, and pressure, the regime established what was usually a tenuous relationship with the Sunni Kurdish population located primarily in the northeastern part of the country.

As one can see, Assad became something of a puppeteer, manipulating the diverse set of groups in the country and often playing them off against one another; indeed, by the time he died in 2000, there were some seventeen different intelligence agencies in Syria with overlapping portfolios that the grand master would utilize to ensure that no one pocket of state authority became too independent or powerful. All of this created a complex and often unseen bureaucratic governing mass.

In addition to all of these horizontal and vertical associations and alliances, the Assad regime established strong relations with the Syrian business class, the majority of whom were Sunni merchants and industrialists. By allowing or arranging for prescribed entrances to personal enrichment through rampant corruption (as much as thirty to forty percent of the economy was based on the black market), Assad was able to co-opt much of the business class into regime maintenance through the implicit understanding that if the regime fell, their economic, social, and political privileges would disappear. Despite all the central planning and state ownership ordained by Baathist ideology, the economy was still by and large dependent upon the private sector. This alliance has often been called the military–merchant complex in Syria, acting as a buffer to the state apparatus. And there were obscure anti-corruption laws on the books the regime would selectively trot out on occasion to target those with whom it was dissatisfied or who posed a threat to the regime. Since the privileged engaged in some level of corruption, everyone was vulnerable, thus guaranteeing a high level of fealty to the regime. As Seale again writes: "The handling of these men, the balancing of one against the other, the way he [Assad] promotes them in turn to his favor as if to head off any possible combination against him, is part of his secret of government."[7] Hafiz al-Assad was certainly not all-powerful. He had to negotiate, manipulate, and bargain with powerful families, tribes, and constituencies in order to get things done, much of which occurred outside his hallowed state institutions. But he was the glue that held it all together.

This is the Syria that Bashar al-Assad, Hafiz's second son, inherited when his father died in June 2000.

7

Bashar al-Assad in Power

Bashar al-Assad took the constitutional oath of office of president and delivered his inaugural speech on July 17, 2000. By Syrian standards, it was a remarkably enlightened speech that deigned even to criticize certain policies of the past, including those of his father. It served to confirm to many in and outside of Syria that Bashar was a breath of fresh air who would lead the country in a new direction. In his speech he made economic reform a clear priority, and while not ruling out democratic reform, he did say that it would have to be "democracy specific to Syria that takes its roots from its history and respects its society."[1] His ascension to power, however, was orchestrated, despite exhortations from Syrian government officials that he was chosen in accordance with the laws and institutions of the state. If this was the case, then Vice President Abd al-Halim Khaddam should have become president. According to various reports, essentially a group of military and security chiefs, led by long-time defense minister and stalwart supporter of the Assads Mustafa al-Tlas, met and decided that it was best for the country – and their own position – that Bashar al-Assad become president. The constitution was even hastily amended, lowering the minimum age a Syrian can become president to thirty-four years old, which just happened to be Bashar's age at the time.

But there was a genuine air of exuberance among many who had longed for change in Syria. Bashar was not originally earmarked for the throne. That was to have been the destiny of his older, more charismatic brother, Basil, who died in a car accident in 1994, at which time Bashar was summoned back to Damascus from London, where he was studying for the equivalent of board certification in ophthalmology at the Western Eye Hospital. His rise in military rank was expedited, and he acquired some important portfolios (such as Lebanon) in what seemed to be a race against time to acquire enough of a loyal support base around him before his ailing father passed away.

Bashar also nurtured a collaborative relationship with elements in the intelligentsia upon his return. These relationships deepened in his capacity as chairman of the Syrian Computer Society. A number of those in his new circles were brought into the government. This added to the anticipatory environment, although the new reformists in the government tended to be technocrats rather than pro-democracy elements. They were tasked with the job of modernizing Syria, implementing administrative reform in the various ministries to which they were assigned, and examining the economic weaknesses of the system and devising ways to correct it; they were not there to enact political reform. Nonetheless, there was noticeably more political openness in the period immediately after Bashar took office. During the seven to eight months of what many have called the "Damascus Spring," the political opening was marked by general amnesties to political prisoners, the licensing of private newspapers, the shaking-up of the state-controlled media apparatus, the allowing of political forums in which open criticism and dissent was tolerated, and the discarding of the personality cult that surrounded Bashar's father.

The regime, however, was caught unawares by the measures implemented by Bashar. Some elements in the regime – whom many have termed the "old guard," those who had reached positions of power under and been loyal to Hafiz al-Assad – basically approached Bashar and warned him of the deleterious effects of the evolving situation in Syria. Serious political reform could jeopardize the predominant position of a number of status quo elements who had established sinecures in the system that had brought them economic, social, and political benefits for years. They had seen the violent end to many of the "old guard" elements in some of the former socialist regimes in Eastern Europe following the conclusion of the superpower cold war. As such, a "Damascus Winter" set in, where the salons were closely monitored or closed, private newspapers were shut down, and democracy activists were arrested.

Although there was still hope, despite this political retraction, that positive change could happen, positive expectations in the West surrounding Bashar al-Assad were unrealistic from the beginning. Just because he was of the younger, modernizing next generation in the Arab world, a licensed ophthalmologist who had studied in London, had an avowed affinity for Western pop music, and was something of a computer nerd, most concluded that he would immediately transform Syria, open it up to the West, and make peace with Israel. They failed to understand the dilapidated, broken-down country he inherited from his father as well as the tumultuous regional and international environments that constricted his ability to implement reform, starting out with the Palestinian al-Aqsa intifada that broke out in September 2000 in the Israeli-occupied territories and caught the attention of the Arab world; followed by the September 11, 2001, terrorist attacks against the United States; and then the US military response first in Afghanistan in October 2001 and then in Iraq in March 2003. Mostly, though, those in the West failed to realize that Bashar was a child of the Arab–Israeli conflict, a child of the superpower cold war, a child of the tumult in Lebanon, and, most importantly, a child of Hafiz al-Assad. These were the events, historical forces, and people who shaped his *Weltanschauung*, not spending eighteen months in London or the music and technological toys of the West. Unfortunately for Bashar al-Assad, when the expectations were high and when he failed to reach them from the perspective of the West, the disappointment and frustration was that much greater.

Despite Syrian intelligence cooperation with the United States following 9/11 regarding al-Qaida, an avowed foe of the secular Baathist, Alawite-dominated regime in Damascus, the administration of US President George W. Bush began to view Syria's traditional support for such groups as Hamas and Hizbullah as no different. Damascus did not adequately adjust to the changes in American foreign policy as a result of 9/11, symbolized by the so-called "Bush doctrine" announced in September 2002. The Syrian regime believed that the old rules of the game in its relationship with the United States were still in place; that despite periods of confrontation in the past, communication was ongoing and future cooperation was still possible. What Damascus did not thoroughly realize was that the new rules of the game were being written in Washington, in the halls of Congress, the Pentagon, and in influential think-tanks, by those who saw Syria as part of the problem rather than part of the solution.

The turning point in this regard came with the US war in Iraq, when Washington accused Damascus of a number of different affronts, including aiding a nascent Iraqi insurgency and sheltering Iraqi fugitives and possibly even the weapons of mass destruction that US personnel could not find in Iraq. Whereas immediately after 9/11, a US State Department official stated that Syria was "saving American lives" amid intelligence cooperation, the perception after the invasion of Iraq was that it was now costing American lives.

The relationship between Damascus and Washington continued to deteriorate despite several trips from US officials to Syria as well as some gestures made by the Syrian regime. This deterioration was symbolized by the passage of the Syrian Accountability Act by Congress in October–November 2003; it was signed into law by President Bush in December. Although mostly symbolic considering the low level of economic interaction between the two countries, the Act provided the president with a range of sanctions against Syria which he could choose to implement. From the perspective of Damascus, however, the US-led coalition in Iraq could easily extend the Bush doctrine to Syria to remove Bashar and his cohorts from power as it had with Saddam Hussein. Anything Syria could do to thwart this possibility, to make the Bush doctrine a one-time deal, was considered fair game; therefore, funneling jihadists through Syria to Iraq in an attempt to ensconce the United States in an Iraqi quagmire was a matter of survival. In addition, as one Syrian security official noted, the Syrians didn't want these jihadists in their own country; in fact, they were surreptitiously hoping US forces would eliminate them once in Iraq. These actions by Syria, though, infuriated Bush administration officials and clearly placed Damascus and Washington at loggerheads.

The pressure on the country began to further mount by the fall of 2004 following what was viewed from the outside as Bashar's blatant intervention in Lebanese politics when Damascus forced upon Beirut the extra-constitutional extension of pro-Syrian President Émile Lahoud's term in office. The international community widely condemned the action, which only fed into the waiting hands of those elements in Washington who wanted to tighten the screws upon the Syrian regime. The United States and France, which led the attack, soon thereafter co-sponsored UN Security Council Resolution 1559, calling for the withdrawal of all foreign forces from Lebanon. Not only had Damascus alienated important European friends, but it had also emboldened a number of important Lebanese figures to more openly call for the withdrawal of Syria's position in Lebanon, not least of whom was former Lebanese prime minister Rafiq Hariri, the billionaire architect of Lebanon's reconstruction following the destructive civil war.

Syria and Lebanon

Bashar was given the Lebanon portfolio by his father in the late 1990s as part of his growing presence in the leadership. It is a very important "file" in the Syrian regime because it oversees extensive Syrian economic, political, and strategic interests. The international community as a whole had been trying to reduce – or eliminate – Syria's footprint in Lebanon, which had been a very deep one indeed since 1975, consecrated by tens of thousands of Syrian troops and a penetrating intelligence apparatus and client network in the country. Even though Bashar had reduced the Syrian troop presence to about four-teen thousand by 2005 (down from about thirty thousand) following Israel's withdrawal from south Lebanon in 2000, nothing really important could get done in Lebanon without the approval of Damascus, especially with the growing power of Hizbullah in the country. So disentangling Syria from Lebanon is easier said than done, as the motto popular in Syria regarding its neighbor to the west, "one people, two countries," clearly indicates. Maintaining influence in Lebanon – or at the very least keeping out elements inimical to Syrian interests – is a strategic necessity from the point of view of Damascus. Dissident ele-ments of previous Syrian regimes housed in Beirut in the first few decades of Syrian independence, even before Israel became involved in Lebanon, were always a constant reminder to Damascus that it needed to have a predominant role in the country. Furthermore, by the 1990s, Lebanon provided Syria with an alternative labor market generating about $2 billion a year in remittances and seasonally employing up to one million Syrians, relieving pressure at home to provide jobs. In addition, once Syria established its footprint in Lebanon, it became a porthole through which well-positioned Syrians could engage in black market and alternative financial/banking activities unavailable to them back home. But because of this very intrusive Syrian posture, opposition in Lebanon to Syria's role there began to mount in the 2000s, especially after the raison d'être of Syria's presence

– namely to protect Lebanon from Israel – was undermined by the Israeli withdrawal.

Syria's position in Lebanon was harmed immeasurably when on February 14, 2005, Rafiq Hariri was assassinated in a massive car bomb explosion in downtown Beirut. Immediately cries rang out in Lebanon and throughout most of the international community holding Syria responsible, either directly or indirectly. Vociferous demonstrations spontaneously erupted in Beirut and other Lebanese cities directly accusing Damascus and its pro-Syrian allies in Lebanon. It was unprecedented open criticism accompanied by calls for Syrian troops and intelligence agents to leave the country. An estimated two hundred thousand people gathered in Beirut for Hariri's funeral procession two days after his death. It was a wildly anti-Syrian crowd, chanting and carrying signs that said such things as "Syria Out!" "No to the hegemony of the Syrian regime and its agents," "It's obvious, no?" and "Bashar, Lahoud, we have prepared coffins for you." The Bush administration was careful not to directly accuse Damascus, preferring not to pass judgment until an internationally sanctioned investigation into the killing ran its course. However, administration officials did publicly hold Syria responsible in a general sense since it was the primary powerbroker in Lebanon. As a sign of Washington's displeasure, the US ambassador to Syria was recalled on the day after the assassination.

Despite some pro-Syrian rallies organized primarily

by Hizbullah, the international pressure relentlessly continued, ultimately compelling Bashar al-Assad to agree to withdraw remaining Syrian forces from Lebanon, which occurred by the end of April 2005. But the UN investigation continued, and on October 21, 2005, the UN report on the assassination of Rafiq Hariri was submitted to the UN Security Council. In the report, Syria was implicated in and found at least indirectly responsible for the murder. The original draft of the report outlined a trail of names that led directly into the heart of the Syrian regime, particularly Asef al-Shawkat, Bashar's head of intelligence and brother-in-law, and Maher al-Assad, his younger brother, who was a member of the Baath Party's central committee and head of the republican guard. The UN Security Council, however, could not agree on concerted action by the end of the year, particularly with Russian and Chinese opposition. In the years that followed, responsibility for the murder focused more on Hizbullah, although, because of its close ties with Damascus, Bashar was not yet out of the woods on this.

The Syrian regime believed, however, that as of mid-2006, it had largely weathered the storm over the Hariri assassination. Washington did not receive the support it had hoped for in the Security Council, and at the same time the US quagmire in Iraq continued amid declining domestic support for the Bush administration policy there. At the same time, Washington's focus seemed to shift over to Iran, with increasing concern that Teheran was in the process of weaponizing its uranium enrichment program toward a nuclear weapons capability. For the time being, then, the spotlight was dimmed considerably on Syria. In the process, Bashar leveraged a strong Syrian nationalistic response to the situation in Lebanon and to UN/US pressure into support for his position and the regime in general. He also used the crisis to move aside potential and real impediments to his authority in Syria, particularly in the summer of 2005 during a regional Baath Party congress meeting when long-time rival Vice President Abd al-Halim Khaddam was compelled to resign. In addition, the Hizbullah–Israeli war in the summer of 2006, which was highly destructive and engulfed half of Lebanon, ended in a stalemate, which, seen in relative terms, was considered something of a victory for Hizbullah. Its leader, Hassan Nasrallah, instantly became wildly popular throughout the Arab world, even among Sunni Muslims. Since Syria was a staunch supporter of Hizbullah and saw itself as a head of what it considered to be an axis of resistance to the "American–Israeli project" in the region, Bashar's position in Damascus and in the region was strengthened by association.

Solidifying Power

In May 2007, amid Bashar's re-election in a referendum to another seven-year term, I noticed something in him that I had not detected before: self-satisfaction.

Maybe this is inevitable in a neopatrimonial author-itarian state, and maybe he was getting his just due after such a tough ride, but ever since I first met him, Bashar had been a very unpretentious, humble leader, even self-deprecating. Despite being surrounded by very serious circumstances, he never seemed to take himself too seriously; indeed, one time I asked him to talk about his biggest accomplishments to date, and he responded that perhaps we should spend more time on his biggest failures. He is not a commanding figure at first glance. He is soft-spoken, gregarious, with an unassuming nature – not the typical profile of a dictator.

The election of 2007 generated tremendous mass support for the re-elected president. Mingling among the throng of supporters around Umayyad Square in Damascus for two days, I could sense that a good portion of this outpouring of affection was genuine. Certainly much was pre-arranged, as in Syria when one group, whether it be a ministry or a private cor-poration, starts to organize celebratory events, others get onboard very quickly, snowballing to create an avalanche of support. Bashar had finally been able to tap into that aquifer of support he had built up, and for the first time he was able to experience it in grand style. It seemed to be a cathartic experience for him after so much that had transpired over the previous two years. He was genuinely touched by the celebra-tions and parades in his honor, and, more importantly, he absorbed it fully.

This was the case even though he ran unopposed in a yes–no referendum vote. Visiting a polling location, I observed that each "voter" had to check the "yes" or "no" box in public amid a band playing and people singing pro-Bashar tunes. The Bashar posters draped over almost every standing structure and out of every window and the "I love Bashar" (in English and Arabic) pins, pendants, and billboards belied his eschewing of such cultish popular behavior to date. Bashar understood that the over ninety-seven percent vote to re-elect him was not an accurate barometer of his real standing in the country. He said it was more important to look at turnout rates for voters, as those who did not vote were more than likely to have voted "no." According to Syrian estimates, the voter turnout rate was seventy-five percent, which was still a very favorable response for Bashar if assessed in this fashion.

This is the first time I felt that Bashar began to believe the sycophants; that to lead the country was his destiny. Maybe it is, but his view of the office had certainly evolved since the early years of his rule. I could see him grow more comfortable with the level of power he had accumulated, and perhaps he had been convinced (or he convinced himself) that the well-being of the country depended on him staying in power. Many have written about the alternative realities that are often constructed around authoritarian leaders; a self-serving bubble that creates a conceptual paradigm of threat and opportunity that is difficult to comprehend from the outside looking in. Considering the trials and tribulations that had abated into a consolidation of power domestically and a less threatening environment regionally, I wondered at the time if Bashar had passed the tipping point in this regard.

By late 2007, he no doubt felt vindicated. Syria was even invited to attend the Annapolis conference the Bush administration sponsored in November that was intended to jumpstart the Middle Eastern peace process. European and Middle Eastern diplomats were beginning to travel to Damascus to meet with Bashar and other Syrian officials. The wall of US-imposed isolation appeared to be crumbling. While not claiming victory outright, Bashar certainly thought that the noose around his neck had been lifted; indeed, time was on *his* side now. Syrians believed they had stayed the course, and it proved to be the correct one. It was the United States that needed to be brought back in from the cold. The 2008 presidential election, with the victory of Democratic candidate Barack Obama in a resounding renunciation of the Bush presidency, allowed the United States – not Syria – an opportunity to make amends.

Navigating the International Arena

Bashar – and Syria – just wanted to be taken seriously by the international community. In a telling exchange that we had in July 2006 during the Hizbullah–Israeli war, I asked the Syrian president what he thought about President Bush's expletive that was inadvertently caught on tape at the G-8 summit meeting earlier in the month. In a conversation with British Prime Minister Tony Blair about the conflict in Lebanon, Bush said, "Yo Blair, you see, the . . . thing is what they need to do is get Syria to get Hizbullah to stop doing this s**t and it's over." Despite the US president's misreading of the influence that Syria actually had over Hizbullah, Bashar's reaction was unexpected and interesting. He said, "I love it. I love that he [Bush] said that. It makes me feel great, because at least he is thinking about Syria. He is thinking about us." Syria was not behind Hizbullah's actions, and Damascus was lucky the Israelis knew that and decided not to take out their wrath against Syria as well. But at least the perception that Syria could wield some damage gave it some utility, some leverage, some more arrows in what had been a near empty quiver.

In late 2008 when I visited Bashar, he certainly believed that he could now sit back and wait to see how things unfolded, such as the policy direction of the new Obama administration as well as the shape of the new Israeli government. He felt empowered politically. It had been a pretty good year for him. There was the Doha Agreement, which enhanced for the time being the Syrian position in Lebanon. French President Nicolas Sarkozy welcomed Bashar in Paris on Bastille Day along with other heads of state – including Israeli Prime Minister Ehud Olmert – signaling a significant breach of the West's attempts to isolate Syria and a major victory for its leader. And perhaps most important of all, the Bush administration was all but gone amid a presidential election that would bring to power someone whose foreign policy philosophy was a direct repudiation of his predecessor's. President Obama indicated in word and action early in his administration that he was favorably disposed toward exploring a dialogue with Damascus. Traditional diplomacy had made a return. Perhaps the old rules of the game would return as well.

However, Syria is indeed weak in relative terms. It can be easily pressured, and there was not much it could do about it at the time. The Israelis struck a suspected Syrian nuclear reactor in September 2007. Hizbullah operations mastermind Imad Mughniyeh was assassinated in a fashionable district of Damascus in February 2008 in what was a very embarrassing incident for the Syrian regime. The United States staged a cross-border raid in October 2008 to kill an alleged Iraqi insurgent with virtual impunity. The response from Damascus to the latter affront was to close the American cultural center and the American School. Not exactly earth-shattering. But Israel and the United States knew Syria could not do much to retaliate in a tit-for-tat manner. Bashar was wise to keep his eye on the ball despite these incidents in terms of not allowing them to spiral out of control or reverse what has been his steady emergence out of the cold.

Although he had consolidated power, Bashar was definitely not all-powerful before the outbreak of the Syrian civil war in 2011. He fought against systemic corruption and an institutional, bureaucratic, and cultural inertia in the country. On many issues, just like his father, he had to negotiate, bargain, and manipulate the system to get things done, and I have witnessed this first hand. Under his father an array of Faustian bargains had been erected whereby unswerving loyalty was pledged in return for casting a blind eye toward personal enrichment. This has the regime sincerely saying and wanting to do one thing while actions by important groups connected to or actually in the regime are sometimes doing something quite different. There is really nothing Bashar can do about it without undercutting his support base, especially in a threatening regional environment when he needs all the friends in and outside of the regime that he can muster. He told me something in October 2008 that provided some insight into his thinking along these lines. We were talking about the potential of elevating the indirect Syrian–Israeli peace negotiations brokered by Turkey that had begun earlier in the year to direct talks with Israel. He said that he really did not want to elevate them without more assurance of success, that he was "new to this game," and since it was his "first time doing this," he "could not afford to fail."

One problem in relations with the United States was that there was still a good bit of left-over anti-Syrian inertia in the Obama administration, in the Pentagon and intelligence community, and in Congress, not to even speak of the negative image of Syria in the minds of the American public. There was also the web of UN resolutions, a UN tribunal on the Hariri assassination, and a sanctions regime erected by the Bush administration that complicated any improvement in US–Syrian relations at the time.

The Syrians were willing to wait it out, play the long game that they believed would inevitably turn in their favor, as it had in the past. After all, they waited out the antipathy of the Bush administration and the repercussions of the Hariri assassination to emerge from the cold. The pressure was off internationally. The fact that Bashar was not traditionally groomed to be president, that he gave up his career to serve his country, won him some breathing space domestically in Syria. The regime, of course, milked this as well to buy him a long learning curve, and he delivered enough change, particularly in the areas of monetary, administrative, and educational reform, to warrant it in the eyes of many, but certainly not all, Syrians. And amid instability in Lebanon, Iraq, and elsewhere in the Middle East, by hook or by crook Bashar had kept Syria relatively stable. Indeed, by the end of 2010 things looked pretty good for Syria and its president. On a trip to Paris in December, Bashar and his wife, Asma, were described as cosmopolitan visitors and were widely photographed in their haute couture clothes, visiting museums, and being hosted by the French elite. Travel magazines touted Syria as a hidden gem for tourism, a stable country replete with unparalleled historical and archeological treasures. Asma herself was featured in a *Vogue* magazine article in March 2011 calling her the "rose of the desert." But this veneer of shine and stability belied the serious socio-economic and political problems that Syria shared with many other countries in the Arab world, which led to an eruption in the region that came to be known as the Arab Spring. And now all bets were off.

8

The Syrian Uprising and Civil War

In late 2010 and early 2011, Syria seemed to be a fairly stable place, especially when compared to Tunisia, Egypt, and Yemen, where events of the so-called "Arab Spring" were beginning to percolate. However, although Bashar al-Assad had improved his own and his country's image, in retrospect his apparent complacency amid the turmoil of the Arab Spring was vividly on display in an interview he gave to journalists from the *Wall Street Journal* in late January 2011.[1] He stated in the interview that the protests in Tunisia, Egypt, and Yemen signaled a "new era" in the Middle East where rulers would need to meet the rising political and economic demands of the people: "If you didn't see the need of reform before what happened in Egypt and Tunisia, it's too late to do any reform." He went on to say that, "Syria is stable. Why? Because you have to be very closely linked to the beliefs of the people. This is the core issue. When there is divergence ... you will have this vacuum that creates disturbances." This was actually a reference to Syria's position on the Israeli–Palestinian issue as well as to Bashar's perceived triumphal resistance to the "American project" in the region. The Syrian president also seemed confident in the level of reform he had implemented in Syria over the years.

Bashar al-Assad was, therefore, probably shocked when the so-called "Arab Spring" uprisings entered his country in force in March 2011. Syrians did not hear a peep from him in the two weeks following the mid-March incidents in the southern city of Deraa, where, reportedly, in response to a number of teenage children having been arrested and tortured by state security for having written anti-regime graffiti on a wall, relatives, friends, and other residents marched out against local authorities demanding redress. It soon devolved into bloodshed as the protestors and government forces clashed, news of which spread like wildfire amidst the heady days of the Arab Spring, and protests and clashes began to pop up in other Syrian towns.

I believe Bashar truly thought he was safe and secure and popular beyond condemnation, so much so that any protests must have been foreign-inspired, which he clearly asserted in his much-awaited – but disappointing – speech to the Syrian parliament on March 30, 2011, the first time he publicly addressed the growing protests. But it was a different Middle East in 2011, where information was now streaming via social media and could not be controlled by authoritarian regimes as it once had been. The perfect storm in the Arab world of higher commodity prices (which made basic items more expensive) and a youth bulge that created an unbridgeable gap between mobilization and assimilation threw into sharp relief the widespread socio-economic problems (especially gross unequal income distribution and growing poverty), corruption, and the restricted political space marked by *mukhabarat*-enforced political repression. In this, Syria was no different. And after the popular uprisings in Tunisia and Egypt led to the removal of the *anciens régimes* in each country, the repressive apparatus could no longer sustain its barrier of fear.

Bashar thought Syria was different. He was obviously wrong. He portrayed his country as almost immune from such domestic unrest. The mouthpieces of the Syrian regime consistently echoed this view, even to the point of expressing support for the protestors in other Arab states. Indeed, calls by anti-Assad elements inside and outside the country for similar protests to be held in Syrian cities in January and February 2011 failed to elicit much of a response, as only a few dozen showed up, rather than the hoped-for thousands who had marched in Tunisian and Egyptian cities. These protests usually fizzled out rapidly or were easily dispersed by security. There just did not seem to be the same energy for opposition in Syria as in other countries, and this only made the regime feel that much more secure.

Bashar's supporters emphasized that the septuagenarian and octogenarian leaders of those other Arab states had been out of touch with their people and had been corrupt lackeys of the United States and Israel. The implication, of course, was that Bashar – who was forty-five years old at the time – was young by comparison and in synch with the Arab youth. He had also consistently confronted the United States and Israel in the region and had supported the resistance forces of Hamas and Hizbullah. He could thus brandish credentials that played well in the Arab street – not only in Syria but throughout the Arab world. This may have bought him some time, but it was a misreading of the situation – or a denial of it. As it turned out, Syria had been suffering from many of the same underlying socio-economic woes that existed in the non-oil-producing Arab countries and that created a well of disenfranchisement and disempowerment, especially among an energized and increasingly frustrated youth.

There were, indeed, more tangible factors that led Bashar and his supporters to believe that they could weather the storm rising in the Arab world, or at least deflect and contain it if it did enter Syria:

(1) Because of the country's turbulent political development following independence in 1946, Syrians have generally disdained engagement in actions that could produce instability. In the decade prior to the Arab Spring they only had to look across their borders, on either side, toward Lebanon and Iraq – two countries that, like Syria, are ethnically and religious diverse – to see how political disorder can violently rip apart the fabric of society. Of course, this trepidation was constantly stoked by the regime to reinforce the necessity of maintaining stability at all costs. It frequently portrayed itself as the only thing standing between order

and chaos. So long as Bashar remained the only viable alternative in the minds of many Syrians, they were not going to participate in an opposition movement that could destabilize the country over the long term. They also feared the brutality of any Syrian government crackdown, with the memory of the massacre in Hama in 1982 within the consciousness of most Syrians (see chapter 6). The repressive apparatus of the state – military, *mukhabarat*, paramilitary groups – was daunting to anyone contemplating taking it on.

(2) The fate of the Syrian military and security services is also closely tied to that of the regime. In contrast to Egypt, these institutions have not been as separate from the political leadership. They aggressively led the violent crackdown of the protestors from the beginning of the uprising. And over his decade-long tenure in power, by 2011 Bashar had successfully manipulated the ruling apparatus, both military and civilian, to have in place an extremely loyal and tight leadership at the top. There have really been remarkably few high-placed defections from the Syrian government when compared to other Arab states convulsed by uprisings.

(3) The minority-ruled Syrian regime, infused as it is with Alawites in important positions, had always represented itself as the protector of all minorities in a country that, as has been noted (chapter 1), is

about sixty-five percent Sunni Arab. In addition to the roughly twelve percent Alawite population, there are various Christian sects comprising about ten percent of the population, plus Druze (around three percent), and a smattering of smaller Shiite sects. The Sunni Kurdish population in Syria (another five to ten percent) have often been a restless and repressed minority under the Assads; however, the Syrian government made a number of concessions to the Kurds, mostly in the area of political autonomy, in the early part of the uprising in order to at the very least keep most of them neutral. The Assads have skillfully played the minority card over the years, practically guaranteeing for themselves at least a twenty to thirty percent support base in the country by playing on fears of the potential for repressive, even fanatical, Sunni Muslim rule and/or instability, in which minorities typically pay a high price. Then there are loyal Sunnis from the business class who had long been co-opted into supporting the regime as well as numerous Sufi Muslim orders in Syria who were actively cultivated by the Assads, especially by Bashar. When all these elements are added together, they account for about half of the Syrian population. For an authoritarian regime, this is not bad: employing coercion, a pervasive spy apparatus, carefully constructed tribal and family alliances, co-optation, and the tactics of divide and rule, maintaining control over the remaining half of the population is not as difficult as it would seem.

(4) Bashar al-Assad himself, prior to the uprising, was generally well liked in the country – or at least not generally reviled. He tended to live modestly and had a popular wife, both of whom were much better at domestic public diplomacy than his father had ever been. The image nurtured was that he and his family were normal – not distanced from the masses but rather aware of and concerned about their problems. Indeed, Bashar's supporters would often talk about him in reverential terms, almost like a prophet delivered to Syria to take the country forward. Of course, this sort of sycophancy only fed Bashar's confidence.

(5) Bashar gained a good bit of credit in the eyes of many Syrians for giving up his passion, ophthalmology, to serve the country when it needed him following his brother's death in 1994 and his father's passing in 2000. Of course, this was promoted as regime propaganda, and it may have bought Bashar a longer learning curve and more public patience with his incremental reform efforts. He was portrayed as having kept the country together despite the external pressures applied against Syria during the previous decade, and in so doing deserving the gratitude of the Syrian people. In addition, there was, indeed, some economic growth, albeit uneven, as well as fiscal, administrative, and education reform that perhaps has been too easily dismissed in the wake of the civil war.

(6) Finally, Syria's internal and external opposition prior to the uprising was often uncoordinated and divided, with no generally recognized leadership, and this carried over into the civil war itself. The Syrian regime had done a good job over the years of ensuring this. There was little if any experience with politics in the opposition because of the restricted political space.

In the end, all of this, while not preventing the protracted civil war, did help Bashar remain in power when many people in and outside of Syria in the early days of the uprising firmly believed he would be the next domino to fall.

Bashar Faces the Protests

There was a great deal of anticipation regarding Bashar's March 30, 2011, speech that addressed the protests publicly for the first time. Many were hoping that the Syrian president would be magnanimous and humble, announcing serious political reforms. This was the moment when Bashar would finally come through, would finally live up to the haughty expectations raised when he first came to power over a decade earlier. They were to be disappointed. Many Syrians in the opposition later identified Bashar's speech as a turning point: their disappointment in the speech made them realize that, in the end, he wasn't any different from his father, and it galvanized the protests. In addition, the fact that Bashar did not punish his cousin, the governor of the province of Deraa, at least as a symbolic gesture in reaction to the civilian deaths there, reinforced the view that any real concessions by the government would be few and far between. A number of Syrian opposition elements from inside the country, both civilian and armed activists, concede that if he had done one or both of these things, the uprising may never have occurred. As one pro-government Hizbullah figure stated:

> Bashar had real popularity in Syria. It was not ninety percent, it was not total or unconditional support, but he had – I think that he had a clear majority who was hoping that Bashar was going to transform the system, little by little. Perhaps some of them were becoming less patient, but when the contestation movement began, if he had taken some measures to directly sanction the guy who tortured the kids in Deraa, if he had taken some anti-corruption measures, even if it was symbolic, it would have made things better. He had to take the decision to confront some clans inside the leadership and the Syrian apparatus and administration and I think that he could have – this kind of measure would have divided the ranks of the contestation, and he would have had a larger popular base.[2]

One Syrian opposition activist frankly stated that Bashar could have remained in power "if he stayed with the Syrian people."[3]

This, in my view, is one of the great tragedies of the conflict: unlike Mubarak in Egypt, Gaddafi in Libya, or even Ben Ali in Tunisia, Bashar al-Assad still enjoyed a level of (perhaps residual) popularity in his country, and he could have possibly rallied the population, if not all of the security forces or the Baath Party leadership, behind him in a more ameliorative direction rather than one of confrontation. It's easy for armchair historians to speculate about this. We are not the ones putting our lives on the line, and undoubtedly there would have been hard-line elements in Damascus who would vigorously oppose any moves by the Syrian president to enact reforms that could undercut their power base; however, it is times like these that separate the great leaders from the also-rans – leaders who might save a country rather than plunging it into the depths and despair of war.

It seems that ultimately Bashar and a critical mass of the Syrian leadership concluded that the battle was on and that the protests had to be eliminated. The regime had to reassert control and stability through force and would play on the penchant of the Syrian population to believe conspiracy theories. And a good many Syrians probably believed them as well; but in the new information age, a growing number of people could no longer be cowed or brainwashed as they had in the past. The Arab Spring had changed the perspectives and the level of demands of ordinary citizens. By blaming unseen forces of conspiracy, the government denied responsibility for (and recognition of) the very real socio-economic and political problems, and ignored the growing clamor of Syrians expressing frustration with the government for lack of accountability, corruption, political repression, and rising poverty. Bashar did not adequately address these issues, which had become much more important to ordinary citizens because they saw in other Arab countries a way to finally combat them.

In the end, convinced by certain elements in his inner circle and security apparatus, Bashar fell back into the default position that the uprising could be taken care of in a matter of weeks. According to one former high-ranking Syrian military figure who was close to the inner circle, "He [Bashar] was tilting on both sides. At some point they [security chiefs] must have told him, move aside, relax, and we'll deal with it."[4] Perhaps this is just the typical response under the Assads. When a domestic threat appears, there is a push-button response of quick and ruthless repression. Survival instincts. No one really questions it. The *mukhabarat* and the elite units of the military swing into action. Maybe the real story in all of this would have been if Bashar had not pressed that button. He probably did not fret over it too much once the initial shock of the protests wore off. This was just how things were done. It was business as usual in the *mukhabarat* state. Bashar became convinced he was actually saving the country from its enemies.

During the first month or two of the uprising, while the regime continued to make some desultory concessions and present an image of calm, the military and security forces intensified their crackdown in cities across Syria. To the outside observer, this approach may seem contradictory and indicative of fissures within the ruling elite on how to respond to the crisis. From the perspective of Bashar and his inner circle, however, it could be seen as two sides of the same coin. In a way that came to be expected of the Assad regimes – old and new – it was something of an axiom of power politics that one never offers concessions from a position of weakness. Therefore, while there was a practical side to the Assad approach, in terms of quelling the unrest, it also clearly indicated that the regime wanted to portray itself as only making concessions and offering reforms from a position of strength. (Indeed, it was actually only re-stating measures previously made so as not to seem as if it was caving in to pressure.) Perhaps the reforms announced could separate the wheat from the chaff of the opposition, thus enabling the regime to land a knockout punch in relatively short order. But, of course, this did not happen.

Ultimately, Bashar al-Assad had little faith that anything other than his continuance in power could lead the way forward. He retrenched and retreated into a typically Syrian authoritarian mode of survival, an Alawite fortress to protect the sect's chokehold on power. In the end, when the pressure was greatest, Bashar was not the enlightened, Western-educated ophthalmologist.

Civil War

The following months saw an exponential increase in violence all over Syria, as the regime crackdown hardened and peaceful protest was abandoned. In response to the regime, the Free Syrian Army (FSA) was formed in the summer of 2011, an amalgam of soldiers who had defected from Syrian armed forces and others seeking an organizational body to coordinate opposition military efforts. Outside of the country, political opposition groups comprised mostly of Syrian exiles established the Syrian National Council (SNC), a civilian body that attempted to become the internationally recognized opposition to the Assad regime. Neither the FSA nor the SNC developed into anything close to what their supporters had envisioned, the former due to fragmentation, lack of coordination, and a dearth of military hardware, and the latter due to the fact that it lacked any legitimacy inside the country from armed opposition groups who were doing the fighting and dying. One of the primary problems of the Syrian conflict early on became evident in these two attempts to form viable opposition bodies: namely that various elements in each were supported by different outside players (such as Saudi Arabia, Qatar, and Turkey), who often had different agendas in terms of who they wanted to support and by what means they wanted to counter the Assad regime.

In fact, by late summer and fall of 2011, when many countries, including the United States, demanded that

Bashar al-Assad step down as president, the conflict had clearly become a proxy war. On the one side, in support of the Syrian government, were Russia, Iran, Hizbullah, and, increasingly, Iraq. The main players arrayed against the Syrian regime, ostensibly in support of various Syrian opposition groups, were the United States and its European allies, Turkey, Saudi Arabia, and Qatar. While the violence and death toll increased, along with the number of Syrian refugees crossing the borders into Turkey, Lebanon, and Jordan, the United Nations arduously worked for a cease-fire. There were some cease-fires on the ground negotiated by the UN (and its special envoy, former UN Secretary-General Kofi Annan), but they were too small-scale and inevitably broke down, especially as the increasing fragmentation of the armed opposition made it almost impossible to implement a truce of any breadth or duration.

The conflict developed into something of a stalemate, where neither side had the wherewithal to secure an outright victory. The regime largely held on to the main cities and immediately surrounding areas, while various opposition groups made gains in the countryside, in small cities and towns, and in the suburbs of some of the main cities. This picture fluctuated from time to time, with the opposition and the regime alternately appearing to be on the uptick. By the summer and fall of 2012, the fighting intensified to the point where one could label the conflict as an all-out civil war. Aleppans reluctantly became ensnared in the conflict by the fall, with the city becoming split between regime forces on one side and opposition groups on the other.

As the conflict deepened, the Syrian opposition, while becoming more fragmented, also became more (Sunni) Islamist. The leading roles in this regard have been played by such groups as Ahrar al-Sham, Jabhat al-Nusra (the al-Qaida affiliate established in early 2012), and ISIS, particularly with the latter's seizure of Raqqa, which became the capital of the self-described Islamic State. There were several factors that fed into this trend. Syria increasingly became a failed state, and typically in such chaos people retreat toward sub-national identities, which in this case meant religious sectarianism (or ethnicity, as in the case of the Kurds, who, with regime acquiescence, carved out semi-autonomous zones in north and northeastern Syria). So as the regime came to be seen largely as the sinecure of Alawite survival, the protector of religious minorities such as Christians, Druze, and other Shiites, and the last bastion of secular diversity, the opposition naturally gravitated toward a more conservative brand of Sunni Islam, better representing the true leanings of an opposition that emerged from a mainly rural and traditional base. Also, since the bulk of financial support from the outside emanated from Sunni conservative countries such as Saudi Arabia, Qatar, and Kuwait, a number of so-called "moderate" or "secular" opposition elements adopted the discourse and style of radical Islamists in order to acquire arms and attract recruits to the cause. Finally, as Syria disintegrated, with life becoming correspondingly less bearable for vast numbers of Syrians, some began to find in radical Sunni Islam a way to make a living as well as a purpose and palliative for their personal, family, and societal suffering.

Of course, this trend made it difficult for Western countries to more assertively back the Syrian opposition for fear that any arms and ammunition supplied to them might find their way into the hands of radical Islamist groups (which did in fact happen on a regular basis), who might then use them against Western interests. In addition, it became more problematic for some countries in the West, especially the United States, to engineer the fall of the Assad regime for fear of the chaos that would ensue, the subsequent spillover effects across Syria's borders, and the probable succession to power of a radical Islamist group such as ISIS.

A case in point was the Obama administration's response to the chemical attacks reportedly carried out by Syrian government forces in the Ghouta area on the edge of Damascus in August 2013 that killed scores of civilians. President Obama had previously said the use of chemical weapons by the Assad regime would be a red line that, if crossed, would, many presumed, elicit a bold military response by the West. It did not happen, perhaps because at the same time the Obama administration was secretly in meetings with Iranian officials that would eventually result in Obama's signature foreign policy success: the deal with Iran to reduce its nuclear footprint. Any military action taken directly against the Syrian government could have derailed the delicate negotiations with Iran. In addition, Obama concluded that Syria was simply much more important to Russia and Iran than the United States; therefore, Bashar's allies would always be willing to do more to help his regime than Washington and its allies would be willing to help the opposition. It was a losing proposition. Instead, Moscow used the hesitation from Washington to insert itself diplomatically, which resulted in a UN-sanctioned agreement for the Syrian government to relinquish, under international supervision, its chemical stockpile and manufacturing facilities. Over the next many months, with a number of stops and starts, it appeared that Damascus met the terms of the agreement.

Bashar al-Assad had to feel at the time as if he might be able to survive after all. He was receiving direct military support from Iran, Hizbullah, and Shiite militias from Iraq and as far afield as Afghanistan. Russia's political and economic support continued, and with the diplomatic intervention of President Vladimir Putin on the chemical weapons deal, its ability to support Syria was enhanced. From the perspective of Damascus, moreover, it appeared that the United States had made the decision that removing Bashar would cause more trouble than it was worth. Finally, the Syrian opposition, despite some gains here and there, still remained more fragmented than not.

The ebb and flow of the war continued. The regime appeared to rebound fairly nicely in late 2014 and early 2015, but it began to experience a series of losses into the spring and summer of 2015 from a variety of fronts. A number of opposition groups, including Jabhat al-Nusra, Ahrar al-Sham, elements of what was left of the FSA, and other smaller militias, combined and coordinated their efforts into a new organization called the Army of Conquest (Jaish al-Fateh). The fact that regional players, such as Saudi Arabia, Turkey, and Qatar, which had supported different (and often competing) Syrian opposition groups to date began to align their support and cooperate more in their joint efforts to remove Bashar certainly helped the cause. The Army of Conquest captured the provincial capital of Idlib (and most of the rest of the Idlib province) and some other strategic spots in northwestern Syria from government forces. On the other side to the east, ISIS forces continued to expand their control of territory in several parts of Syria, and most spectacularly, as noted above (chapter 1), took the city of Palmyra, home to incomparable Roman ruins, some of which were then destroyed.

The Syrian regime was on its heels. Evidence of this was a speech given by Bashar al-Assad in July 2015 in which he admitted for the first time that the government was running low on manpower and resources. Until then, the regime always presented itself as the only entity in the war that could reconstitute Syria again and restore stability. In the speech, however,

Bashar admitted that, at least in the short term, government forces would not be able to regain lost territory. Once again, prognosticators had the regime on its last legs, losing as much from attrition as anything else.

Again, the prognosticators would be wrong. This time it wasn't the unexpected resilience of regime forces or significantly more Iranian or Hizbullah troops. It was the Russians. On September 30, 2015, Russia began a sustained air campaign against Syrian opposition positions from an airbase it built outside of Latakia. In essence, Russia became the Syrian air force. As a result, Syrian and pro-government forces were able to go on the offensive and retake some territory (including Palmyra in March 2016 and Aleppo by the end of the year). Combined with the shrinking territory held by ISIS, including the fall of Raqqa in 2017 to the US-supported Syrian Democratic Front (SDF), composed mostly of Syrian Kurds, the military successes by Russian- and Iranian-supported regime forces well into 2018 made it seem that the only side that produced something resembling victory was the Syrian government.

With the military intervention, Putin made an emphatic statement, basically saying to those countries which had been supporting various Syrian opposition groups that Russia was not going to let the Syrian regime of Bashar al-Assad collapse. Moscow preserved its strategic interests in Syria and also secured a central role for itself in any sort of negotiated settlement to the conflict. If successful, Putin would stand tall, rehabilitate Russia's image following its military adventure in the Ukraine, and perhaps a grateful Europe, itself reeling under the weight of thousands of Syrian refugees flooding into the continent, would bring to an end the international economic sanctions imposed on Moscow.

The Russian military intervention did, in fact, reactivate a scattered process of diplomacy, with the UN sponsoring one track in Geneva; Russia, Iran, and Turkey sponsoring the Astana (Kazakhstan) process; and a Russian-hosted track convening Syrian government and Syrian opposition groups. It all appeared uncoordinated, if not counterproductive. There were some de-escalation agreements, de-confliction accords, and humanitarian corridors established, but the drumbeat of war continued on despite all this, with the Syrian government determined to recapture as much territory as possible – and doing so; indeed, Bashar stated in June 2018 that he expected the war to be over in less than a year.

The narrative regarding Bashar al-Assad also began to shift, as many of the anti-Assad states began to show more flexibility on whether or not the Syrian president had to vacate office during or immediately following a transition process (as outlined in the Geneva II communiqué of June 2012). With the defeat of ISIS, however, a power vacuum was created in Syria, with a host of stakeholders racing to ensure that their strategic objectives in the country were secured. While doing so, an array of competing military forces were on the ground in close proximity to one another. And they were starting to run into each other – with deadly results. By early 2018, Turkey had launched another offensive in northern Syria to roll back Kurdish gains amid tensions with the United States, which had been supporting Kurdish elements against ISIS, groups (such as the People's Protection Units or YPG) that Turkey considers terrorists; US forces clashed with Russian contract military trying to advance regime control in the Euphrates region, reportedly killing hundreds of Russian troops; Israel shot down an Iranian drone and then carried out a significant attack against Syrian and Iranian bases from which the drone originated; and in response to the shooting down of one of their jets by Syrian surface-to-air missile batteries, the Israelis responded with a massive retaliatory strike that may have destroyed half of Syria's missile defense system. To say the least, it was a very dangerous situation that threatened to spiral out of control into a regional or even international conflict if the parties were not careful. Russia itself by summer 2018 was mediating between the Iranians and the Israelis in an attempt to separate forces and prevent military mishaps.

By mid-2018, the Syrian government continued to extend its authority over territory that had been lost, particularly around Damascus and in the south along the Jordanian border and the Golan Heights. It was a symbolic victory for Damascus to be able to re-take Deraa, the birthplace of the uprising, during the summer. The province of Idlib in the northwest was the only significant region still under largely opposition control. No doubt the Syrian government has its eyes set on re-taking it as well. It is clear to most observers that Bashar al-Assad plans to remain in power until his current term in office expires in 2021 and possibly even beyond. The improved military fortunes of the Syrian government also convinced most countries that supported the opposition to accept Bashar as president of Syria in the near if not long term. But the patronage network the Assads meticulously built over forty years has been smashed. A whole new set of relationships must be established by the regime with a population, even those who remained loyal to the government during the war, that has been empowered by living without the Syrian state for years. One wonders if the Syrian leadership can navigate this moving forward.

Time will tell if Syria can be rebuilt. Syrians face enormous challenges, not least of which is the fact there is an estimated $300 billion of reconstruction needed. As noted in chapter 1, it is estimated that as of mid-2018 about five hundred thousand Syrians have been killed in the war, with over half the population either internally or externally displaced. More than eighty percent of Syrians live below the poverty line. The unemployment rate is approaching sixty percent, with many of those working being employed in the war economy as smugglers, fighters, or arms dealers. Life expectancy has dropped by twenty years since the beginning of the uprising, with about half of the children in Syria no longer attending school – a lost generation. The country has become a public health disaster, with diseases formerly under control, like typhoid, tuberculosis, hepatitis A, and cholera, once again endemic.[5] And on and on.

Syrians, however, are a resilient people. As outlined in this book, the country has endured and survived many challenges over the course of its modern history. This is, perhaps, the biggest challenge to date. It may take a generation, but with a healthy dose of compassion and empathy on all sides, maybe reconciliation and rebuilding, rather than revenge, can take place. One must remember that not only material reconstruction is needed but also emotional reconstruction after so much blood has been spilt. But in the end, I will bet on the Syrians.

Further Reading

There is a healthy – and growing – literature on modern Syria. A good place to start is with *The Levant: Fractured Mosaic* (Princeton: Markus Wiener Publishers, 2008) by William Harris. This book helps situate Syria within its Levantine historical context from ancient times to the present.

At a more specific level, books that examine Syria in whole or in part during the period of Ottoman rule from 1517 to World War I are the following: George Antonius' *The Arab Awakening* (New York: G. P. Putnam's Sons, 1979); C. Ernest Dawn's *From Ottomanism to Arabism: Essays on the Origin of Arab Nationalism* (Urbana-Champaign: University of Illinois Press, 1973); Dick Douwes' *The Ottomans in Syria: A History of Justice and Oppression* (London: I. B. Tauris, 2000); Philip S. Khoury's *Urban Notables and Arab Nationalism: The Politics of Damascus, 1860–1920* (Cambridge: Cambridge University Press, 1983); Abraham Marcus' *The Middle East on the Eve of Modernity: Aleppo in the Eighteenth Century* (New York: Columbia University Press, 1989); Abdul-Karim Rafeq, Peter Sluglet, and Stefan Weber (eds.), *Syria and Bilad al-Sham under Ottoman Rule* (Leiden: E. J. Brill, 2010); and A. L. Tibawi's *American*

Interests in Syria, 1800–1901 (Oxford: Clarendon Press, 1966).

The standard work on the French Mandate in Syria is Philip S. Khoury's *Syria and the French Mandate: The Politics of Arab Nationalism, 1920–1945* (Princeton: Princeton University Press, 1987). There is also Stephen H. Longrigg's *Syria and Lebanon under the French Mandate* (Oxford: Oxford University Press, 1958). Books that deal with more specific episodes during this period are the following: David Fromkin's *A Peace to End All Peace* (New York: Henry Holt and Company, 1989), which examines the diplomacy regarding the Middle East in World War I; James Gelvin's *Divided Loyalties: Nationalism and Mass Politics in Syria at the Close of Empire* (Berkeley: University of California Press, 1998); and Michael Provence's *The Great Syrian Revolt and the Rise of Arab Nationalism* (Austin: University of Texas Press, 2005).

Two classic books examine the post-independence period in Syria in the 1950s heading into the Arab cold war in the 1960s: Malcolm H. Kerr's *The Arab Cold War: Gamal 'Abd al-Nasir and His Rivals, 1958–1970* (London: Oxford University Press, 1971); and Patrick Seale's *The Struggle for Syria: A Study of Post-War Arab Politics, 1945–1958* (new edition; New Haven: Yale University Press, 1987). Other books dealing with various aspects of this period, including the rise of the Baath Party, are: John Devlin's *The Ba'th Party: A History of Its Origins to 1966* (Stanford: Hoover Institution Press, 1976); Rami Ginat's

Syria and the Doctrine of Arab Neutralism (Brighton: Sussex Academic Press, 2005); Steven Heydemann's *Authoritarianism in Syria: Institutions and Social Conflict, 1946–1970* (Ithaca, NY: Cornell University Press, 1999); Raymond Hinnebusch's *Syria: Revolution from Above* (London: Routledge, 2002); David W. Lesch's *Syria and the United States: Eisenhower's Cold War in the Middle East* (Boulder, CO: Westview Press, 1992); Sami M. Moubayed's *Damascus between Democracy and Dictatorship* (Lanham, MD: University Press of America, 2000); Gordon Torrey's *Syrian Politics and the Military, 1945–1958* (Columbus: Ohio State University Press, 1964); and for an examination of the United Arab Republic, see Elie Podeh's *The Decline of Arab Unity: The Rise and Fall of the United Arab Republic* (Brighton: Sussex Academic Press, 1999).

For Syria under Hafiz al-Assad, the following book is especially recommended: Patrick Seale's *Asad of Syria: The Struggle for the Middle East* (Berkeley: University of California Press, 1988), which is the most comprehensive biography of the Syrian president to the late 1980s. In addition are the following: J. K. Gani's *The Role of Ideology in Syrian–US Relations* (Basingstoke: Palgrave Macmillan, 2014); Raymond Hinnebusch's *Authoritarian Power and State Formation in Ba'thist Syria: Army, Party, and Peasant* (Boulder, CO: Westview Press, 1990); Moshe Maoz's *Asad: The Sphinx of Damascus* (London: Weidenfeld & Nicolson, 1988); Volker Perthes' *The Political Economy of Syria under Asad* (London: I. B. Tauris, 1995); Nikolaos van Dam's *The Struggle for Power in Syria: Politics and Society under Asad and the Ba'th Party* (fourth edition; London: I. B. Tauris, 2011); Lisa Wedeen's *Ambiguities of Domination: Politics, Rhetoric, and Symbols in Contemporary Syria* (Chicago: University of Chicago Press, 1999); and Eyal Zisser's *Asad's Legacy in Transition* (London: Hurst, 2001).

Since 2011, books on Syria have understandably focused on the civil war. As a consequence, there are but few worthy books that focus on Bashar's first decade in power: Alan George's *Syria: Neither Bread nor Freedom* (London: Zed Books, 2003) is a scathing critique of Syria under his rule; and David W. Lesch's *The New Lion of Damascus: Bashar al-Asad and Modern Syria* (New Haven: Yale University Press, 2005) offers a more sympathetic portrayal of his first years in power. Other accounts include: Flynt Leverett's *Inheriting Syria: Bashar's Trial by Fire* (Washington, DC: Brookings Institute Press, 2005); Volker Perthes' *Syria under Bashar al-Asad: Modernization and the Limits of Change* (Oxford: Oxford University Press, 2004); and Eyal Zisser's *Commanding Syria: Bashar al-Asad and the First Years in Power* (London: I. B. Tauris, 2007).

There was a spate of books that were published in the early years of the Syrian civil war. Among them were: Fouad Ajami's *The Syrian Rebellion* (Stanford: Hoover Institution Press, 2012); Emile Hokayem's *Syria's Uprising and the Fracturing of the Levant* (London: Routledge, 2013); David W. Lesch's *Syria: The Fall of the House of Assad* (New Haven:

Yale University Press, 2013); Stephen Starr's *Revolt in Syria: Eyewitness to the Uprising* (New York: Columbia University Press, 2012); Andrew Tabler's *In the Lion's Den: An Eyewitness Account of Washington's Battle with Syria* (Chicago: Lawrence Hill Books, 2011); and Samar Yazbek's *A Woman in the Crossfire: Diaries of the Syrian Revolution* (London: Haus Publications, 2012). A few more have been published recently and are updated accounts. The most notable ones are: Samer N. Abboud's *Syria* (Cambridge: Polity, 2018); Raymond Hinnebusch and Omar Imady (eds.), *The Syrian Uprising: Domestic Origins and Early Trajectory* (London: Routledge, 2018); Christopher Phillips' *The Battle for Syria: International Rivalry in the New Middle East* (New Haven: Yale University Press, 2016); and Nikolaos van Dam's *Destroying a Nation: The Civil War in Syria* (London: I. B. Tauris, 2017).

There are a few books that transcend specific time periods in Syria's modern history that are worth a look: Richard T. Antoun and Donald Quataert (eds.), *Syria: Society, Culture, and Polity* (New York: State University of New York Press, 1991); Moshe Maoz, Joseph Ginat, and Onn Winckler (eds.), *Modern Syria: From Ottoman Rule to Pivotal Role in the Middle East* (Brighton: Sussex Academic Press, 1999); and Sami M. Moubayed's *Steel and Silk: Men and Women Who Shaped Syria, 1900–2000* (Seattle: Cune Press, 2006). There is a beautiful and very informative memoir written by Elaine Rippey Imady, who married a Syrian man in the late 1950s and moved to Syria from the

United States. She tells her remarkable story in *Road to Damascus* (Hollister, CA: MSI Press, 2008). Finally, as a general reference to Syrian people, terms, places, and historical events (including an extensive bibliography), see David Commins and David W. Lesch's *Historical Dictionary of Syria* (Lanham, MD: Scarecrow Press, 2014).

Notes

Chapter 1: What is Syria?

1　Christopher Phillips, *Everyday Arab Identity: The Daily Reproduction of the Arab World* (London: Routledge, 2016).
2　William Harris, *The Levant: A Fractured Mosaic* (Princeton: Markus Wiener Publishers, 2005), pp. 1–2.
3　Ibid., p. 2.
4　Nikolaos van Dam, *The Struggle for Power in Syria: Politics and Society under Asad and the Ba'th Party* (fourth edition; London: I. B. Tauris, 2011), pp. 6–7.
5　Ibid., p. 9.
6　Patrick Seale, *Asad of Syria: The Struggle for the Middle East* (Berkeley: University of California Press, 1988), p. 8.

Chapter 2: World War I

1　David Fromkin, *A Peace to End All Peace* (New York: Henry Holt and Company, 1989), p. 95.
2　Ibid., p. 13.
3　Quoted in ibid., p. 330.

Chapter 3: The French Mandate

1　Philip Khoury, *Syria and the French Mandate: The Politics of Arab Nationalism, 1920–1945* (Princeton: Princeton University Press, 1987), p. 4.
2　Ibid., pp. 104–5.
3　Ibid., p. 620.
4　C. Ernest Dawn, *From Ottomanism to Arabism: Essays on the Origins of Arab Nationalism* (Urbana-Champaign: University of Illinois Press, 1973).

5 Sami Moubayed, *The Makers of Modern Syria: Rise and Fall of Syrian Democracy, 1918–1958* (London: I. B. Tauris, 2018), p. 38.

Chapter 4: Syria amid the Cold Wars

1 Patrick Seale, *The Struggle for Syria: A Study in Post-War Arab Politics, 1945–1958* (new edition; New Haven: Yale University Press, 1987).
2 Foreign Office Report, "Syria: Annual Report for 1956," November 15, 1957, FO 371/128219, Public Record Office (PRO), Kew Gardens, London.
3 For a range of views on the Syrian response to the Eisenhower doctrine, see Weekly Letter on Syria and Egypt, British Embassy–Beirut, February 15, 1957, FO 371/128221, PRO; and DA Intelligence Reports, January 22, 1957, Entry 85, Intell. Doc. File, R-27-57 and R-28-57, Record Group 319, National Archives and Records Administration (NARA), Suitland, Maryland.
4 DA Intelligence Report, February 19, 1957, Entry 85, Intell. Doc. File, 2040561, Record Group 319, NARA.
5 For a detailed analysis of this crisis, see David W. Lesch, *Syria and the United States: Eisenhower's Cold War in the Middle East* (Boulder, CO: Westview Press, 1992).
6 For more on Nasser's efforts in the American–Syrian crisis, see David W. Lesch, "Gamal Abd al-Nasser and an Example of Diplomatic Acumen," *Middle Eastern Studies* 31, no. 2 (1995), pp. 362–74.

Chapter 5: The 1967 Arab–Israeli War

1 Quoted in Tom Segev, *1967: Israel, the War, and the Year that Transformed the Middle East* (New York: Metropolitan Books, 2005), pp. 191–2.
2 The shift in power in Syria from the National to the Regional Command can be traced back to a Regional Command Baath Party congress of September 1963 and a National Command Baath Party congress meeting the following month, when the

party's founders, Aflaq and Bitar, were marginalized in the Regional Command. They were replaced by younger officers of rural, peasant origins, many of whom were Alawite or Druze, including the Alawite Major-General Salah Jadid, who would become the strongman in Syria following the February 1966 coup. Along with Jadid, another military Baathist, Hafiz al-Assad, entered the power structure as part of the Military Committee of the Baath Party and later became minister of defense when Jadid came to power.

3 For instance, see van Dam, *The Struggle for Power in Syria*; and Raymond A. Hinnebusch, *Authoritarian Power and State Formation in Ba'thist Syria: Army, Party and Peasant* (Boulder, CO: Westview Press, 1990).

4 Malcolm H. Kerr, *The Arab Cold War: Gamal 'Abd al-Nasir and His Rivals, 1958–1970* (London: Oxford University Press, 1971), pp. 118–19.

5 Seale, *Asad of Syria*, p. 104.

6 Ibid., p. 123.

7 Fuad Jabber, "The Resistance Movement before the Six Day War," in William B. Quandt, Fuad Jabber, and Ann Moseley Lesch, *The Politics of Palestinian Nationalism* (Berkeley: University of California Press, 1973), p. 174.

8 Quoted in Segev, *1967*, p. 195.

9 Quoted in van Dam, *The Struggle for Power in Syria*, p. 57. Hatum returned to Syria during the 1967 June war ostensibly to fight for his country. He was summarily arrested, tried by a special military court, and was executed on June 24.

10 Fred H. Lawson, *Why Syria Goes to War: Thirty Years of Confrontation* (Ithaca, NY: Cornell University Press, 1996), p. 44.

11 Ibid., pp. 39–41.

12 Ibid., p. 42.

13 It is interesting that in US government correspondence through May 18, the crisis and potential war were seen as an Israeli–Syrian affair, not as Egyptian. That would soon change, especially when Nasser announced the closure of the Strait of Tiran on May 22. For instance, see Memorandum from the President's Special Assistant (Rostow) to President

Johnson, May 15, 1967, *Foreign Relations of the United States* (FRUS), Volume XIX, Doc. No. 4; and Telegram from the Embassy in Jordan to the Department of State, May 18, 1967, FRUS, Volume XIX, Doc. No. 12.

14 Quoted in Seale, *Asad of Syria*, p. 130.

15 Michael B. Oren, *Six Days of War: June 1967 and the Making of the Modern Middle East* (New York: Ballantine Books, 2003), p. 292.

16 Quoted in ibid., p. 292.

17 Mustafa Tlas, *Mir'at Hayati* [The Mirror of My Life], Part 2, *1958–1968* (Damascus: Dar Tlas, 1995), p. 874.

18 Memorandum of Conversation, June 28, 1967, FRUS, Volume XIX, Doc. No. 331.

Chapter 6: Syria under Hafiz al-Assad

1 Steven Heydemann, "The Political Logic of Economic Rationality: Selective Stabilization in Syria," in Henri Barkey (ed.), *The Politics of Economic Reform in the Middle East* (New York: St. Martin's Press, 1992), pp. 11–39. On Syria's political economy, see Volker Perthes, *The Political Economy of Syria under Asad* (London: I. B. Tauris, 1995), or, for a more brief treatment, see David W. Lesch, "Is Syria Ready for Peace? Obstacles to Integration in the Global Economy," *Middle East Policy*, vol. VI, no. 3 (February 1999), pp. 93–111.

2 In return, Syria received tacit recognition within the Arab world and by the United States of its predominant role in Lebanon. Syria's position was cemented with its "Friendship and Cooperation" agreement with the government in Beirut in May 1991.

3 For details on the Israeli–Syrian negotiations through 1995–6, see Itamar Rabinovich, *The Brink of Peace: The Israeli–Syrian Negotiations* (Princeton: Princeton University Press, 1998), and Uri Savir, *The Process: 1,100 Days That Changed the Middle East* (New York: Random House, 1998).

4 Hisham Sharabi, *Neopatriarchy: A Theory of Distorted Change in Arab Society* (London: Oxford University Press), p. 7.

5 Ibid.

6 Patrick Seale, "Asad: Between Institutions and Autocracy," in Richard T. Antoun and Donald Quataert (eds.), *Syria: Society, Culture, and Polity* (New York: State University of New York Press, 1991), p. 103.

7 Ibid., p. 105.

Chapter 7: Bashar al-Assad in Power

1 This chapter is in part based upon the author's work *The New Lion of Damascus: Bashar al-Asad and Modern Syria* (New Haven: Yale University Press, 2005) and personal meetings with President Assad between 2004 and 2009.

Chapter 8: The Syrian Uprising and Civil War

1 Jay Soloman and Bill Spindle, "Syria Strongman: Time for Reform," *Wall Street Journal*, January 31, 2011.

2 Interview with Hizbullah figure, Beirut, August 2013, Harvard–NUPI–Trinity University Syria Research Project (HNT). This project focused on meeting with top officials in most of the stakeholder countries and groups involved in the Syrian conflict in 2012 and 2013. A final report was published in fall 2013 and made available to the UN, the sponsoring parties, and select governments. An abridged version of the report, "Obstacles to a Resolution of the Syrian Conflict," can be found at the following site: https://www.belfercenter.org/publication/obstacles-resolution-syrian-conflict

3 Interview with Syrian opposition activist, Gaziantep, Turkey, December 2012, HNT.

4 Interview with former high-level Syrian military figure, February 2013, HNT.

5 See David W. Lesch and James Gelvin, "Assad Has Won in Syria. But Syria Hardly Exists," *The New York Times*, January 11, 2017.

Index

Printed and bound by CPI Group (UK) Ltd, Croydon, CR0 4YY

09/06/2025

14685748-0001